STAYING
AT THE
TABLE

STAYING AT THE TABLE

THE GIFT OF UNITY
FOR UNITED METHODISTS

Scott J. Jones

Abingdon Press
Nashville

Library of Congress Cataloging-in-Publication Data

Staying at the table: the gift of unity for United Methodists / edited by Scott J. Jones.
  p. cm.
  Includes bibliographical references.
  ISBN 978-0-687-64506-0 (binding: pbk., adhesive perfect: alk. paper)
1. Concord.   2. United Methodist Church (U.S.)—Doctrines.   I. Jones, Scott J.

BV4647.C6S73   2007
287'.6—dc22   2007031617

All scripture quotations unless noted otherwise are taken from the New Revised Standard Version of the Bible, copyright 1989, Division of Christian Education of the National Council of the Churches of Christ in the United States of America. Used by permission. All rights reserved.

References to *The Book of Discipline* are from *The Book of Discipline of The United Methodist Church* © 2004 by The United Methodist Publishing House. Used by permission.

Excerpt from "Little Gidding" in FOUR QUARTERS, copyright 1942 by T.S. Eliot and renewed 1970 by Esme Valerie Eliot, reprinted by permission of Harcourt, Inc.

Excerpt from "The Second Coming" by William Butler Yeats. Used by permission of A P Watt Ltd on behalf of Gráinne Yeats.

Reprinted with the permission of Scribner, an imprint of Simon & Schuster Adult Publishing Group, from THE COLLECTED WORKS OF W.B. YEATS, VOLUME I: THE POEMS, Revised, edited by Richard J. Finneran. Copyright © 1924 by The Macmillan Company; copyright renewed © 1952 by Bertha Georgie Yeats. All rights reserved.

Excerpt by Martin Luther King, Jr. reprinted by arrangement with the Heirs to the Estate of Martin Luther King, Jr. c/o Writers House as agent for the proprietor, New York, NY.

Copyright 1963 Martin Luther King, Jr., copyright renewed 1991 Corretta Scott King.

08 09 10 11 12 13 14 15 16 17—10 9 8 7 6 5 4 3 2 1

MANUFACTURED IN THE UNITED STATES OF AMERICA

CONTENTS

PREFACE

Conversations about the unity of Christ's church have been important since New Testament times. After many divisions of the church down through the centuries, movements toward unity gathered momentum in the twentieth century. Now, a number of Christian denominations are facing pressures and tensions that lead some to believe the cause of Christianity would be better served by splitting the churches apart. And it appears that we in our United Methodist Church are in the midst of a pivotal discussion about our unity. These are difficult times for The United Methodist Church. However, it is my conviction, as a bishop of the Church, that we need to focus on how we can find common ground in "the extreme center." It is also my conviction that unity is a gift from God.

My perspective is also shaped, in part, by an image from William Butler Yeats's "The Second Coming":

> Turning and turning in the widening gyre
> The falcon cannot hear the falconer;
> Things fall apart; the center cannot hold;
> Mere anarchy is loosed upon the world,
> The blood-dimmed tide is loosed and everywhere
> The ceremony of innocence is drowned;
> The best lack all conviction, while the worst are full of passionate intensity.[1]

1. Reprinted with the permission of Scribner, an imprint of Simon & Schuster Adult Publishing Group, from THE COLLECTED WORKS OF W.B. YEATS, VOLUME I: THE POEMS, Revised, edited by Richard J. Finneran. Copyright © 1924 by The Macmillan Company; copyright renewed © 1952 by Bertha Georgie Yeats. All rights reserved.

Since writing this poem, Yeats has been proved both partially right and partially wrong. In many ways, the center has held during the last one hundred years in the fields of politics, international relations, business, and religion. But he was prophetic enough to note the incredible dangers and tendencies of the last century when things did fall apart, and the center did not hold. Let us take his image as a warning for us. The strength of Wesleyan doctrine is its ability to articulate a holistic, balanced, and practical interpretation of Scripture. It is conservative in some ways and liberal in other ways; it occupies the extreme center and is totally opposed to the dead center.

This book offers one bishop's view of what truly constitutes Christian unity and why it is important. While most of my views are applicable to Christians generally, I wish to speak specifically to my own Church with reference to our own issues. In preparation for the General Conference of 2008, but also in preparation for the entire future of the Church, I hope to suggest wherein our unity lies and some ideas of how we might live more fully into God's gift of unity.

But I seek not only to talk about unity but also to model it. Thus, I have invited a diverse group of Church leaders to read and reflect on my essay. Their responses are included as part of the book. In a sense, this is a dialogue between me and each contributor. It is also a kind of symposium on the future of The United Methodist Church. While the respondents I chose are diverse in many ways, they are also thoughtful people and care deeply about the Church. I am truly grateful to them for their willingness to engage in the conversation.

I love the Church of Jesus Christ, and as a leader, I have a responsibility to help our Church follow where God leads. And just as important, I want our Church to be faithful disciples participating in God's mission to the end that God's reign might come on earth as it is in heaven. This, after all, is the purpose of God's gift of unity for us.

CHAPTER ONE

GOD'S GIFT OF UNITY FOR UNITED METHODISM

U nity is God's gift, and Christians should claim it.

The United Methodist Church should not split. Nor should its leaders allow it to be torn apart. Nor should anyone let herself or himself so focus on one part of the Church's life or mission that the gospel beauty and excellence of the whole is ruined.

The General Conference of 2004 was a tumultuous time. Prior to the meeting, several persons, both liberal and conservative, had written or spoken in ways that suggested it was time for the Church to think about splitting. Sometimes those proposals suggested that an opposing group should leave the Church. Other times, the weariness and frustration of dealing with controversial issues led some to say they were ready to leave the Church. During the Conference a group of persons began talking, and ideas about amicable separation were put on paper. Following the revelation of a written proposal for splitting the Church, the Conference reacted.

On May 7, 2004, the Conference supported a resolution brought by six persons—one from each jurisdiction in the United States and from one Central Conference—stating the Church's commitment to unity. Approved overwhelmingly, the resolution said,

> As United Methodists, we remain in covenant with one another, even in the midst of disagreement, and affirm our commitment to work

together for a common mission of making disciples of Jesus Christ throughout the world.[1]

In this way the question of the continuing unity of The United Methodist Church took a new turn and received a new urgency. This was not a new conversation. Many such discussions have occurred both formally and informally for many years. Most notably, the conclusions of a dialogue on unity sponsored by the General Commission on Christian Unity and Interreligious Concerns were published as a document, "In Search of Unity," that sought to clarify many of the issues.[2] While for many this is primarily a debate about homosexuality, "In Search of Unity" identified deeper issues. It argued that strong disagreements within the church on Christology, ecclesiology, and the authority of Scripture were the main problems and that the debate on homosexuality was a symptom of deeper disagreements. They said,

> There are many ways in which the unity of our church has come under strain over the years. Some of the factors at work are easy to identify; some are not. Some are relatively isolated and independent; others are deeply intertwined in complex and even enigmatic ways. It is useful to distinguish between three kinds of challenges to unity: 1) Some challenges are those that we associate with the human condition (the fall from original righteousness); 2) Other challenges extend from disagreements that harm the quality of our existence in a variety of ways; and 3) Yet other challenges run so deep as to harbor the danger of explicit disunity or schism.[3]

As the next General Conference prepares to meet, I hope to contribute to the continuing conversation about how best to think about and receive the gift of unity.

In addition to the issues addressed in the dialogue about unity quoted above, there is another question of unity facing the Church. In many ways, The United Methodist Church is a global Church. It is one body, with one mission, one set of doctrinal standards, and one Council of Bishops. It has general agencies with ministries that affect the entire Church and local congregations meeting and serving in more than fifty countries on four continents. Yet, the Church continues to function like a United States Church with a few non-U.S. outposts. Since 1964 various committees and task forces have addressed the issue of the global nature of The United Methodist Church, so the ongoing conversation about the global nature of our Church will be part of the discussion here.

The Vision of the New Testament and the Early Church

The New Testament clearly envisions that some degree of unity will exist among all of the disciples of Jesus. Jesus prayed,

> "I ask not only on behalf of these, but also on behalf of those who will believe in me through their word, that they may all be one. As you, Father, are in me and I am in you, may they also be in us, so that the world may believe that you have sent me." (John 17:20-21)

When the church was facing a variety of tensions, Paul advised them,

> I therefore, the prisoner in the Lord, beg you to lead a life worthy of the calling to which you have been called, with all humility and gentleness, with patience, bearing with one another in love, making every effort to maintain the unity of the Spirit in the bond of peace. There is one body and one Spirit, just as you were called to the one hope of your calling, one Lord, one faith, one baptism, one God and Father of all, who is above all and through all and in all. (Ephesians 4:1-6)

Paul goes so far as to say, "As many of you as were baptized into Christ have clothed yourselves with Christ. There is no longer Jew or Greek, there is no longer slave or free, there is no longer male and female; for all of you are one in Christ Jesus" (Galatians 3:27-28). By the time of the Councils of Nicaea and Constantinople in the fourth century, these scriptural teachings had been summarized in the third article of the creed: "We believe in the one holy catholic and apostolic church."[4]

These texts—Jesus' prayer in John 17, Ephesians 4, Galatians 3, and the Nicene Creed—are worthy of extended commentary and exposition. Such a commentary would find many ways to elaborate on a basic theme of the gospel: it is God's will that all of the disciples of Jesus be one. To the extent that we are separated from each other, or, even worse, in conflict with one another, we are in rebellion against God's will for God's Church.

But what sort of unity is it that God wills for us? God values diversity.[5] Again, the New Testament gives many strong indications that God does not intend uniformity. Two key texts show this. First, on the day of Pentecost, the Holy Spirit descended on the disciples and they began speaking in different languages. Acts 2:5-6 says, "Now there were devout Jews from every nation under heaven living in Jerusalem. And at this sound the crowd gathered and was bewildered, because each one heard them speaking in the native language of each." If the Holy Spirit had worked a miracle so that all of the listeners could suddenly speak and understand Aramaic or even Hebrew that would have been an indication of movement toward uniformity. Instead, the Spirit worked so that each person heard Peter's message in his or her own language.

The other crucial text supporting diversity is Paul's image of the church as a body. The church at Corinth was suffering from a number of divisions—based on who was baptized by whom or spiritual gifts or wealth and perhaps other factors—which Paul addressed in the twelfth chapter of 1 Corinthians:

> For just as the body is one and has many members, and all the members of the body, though many, are one body, so it is with Christ. For in the one Spirit we were all baptized into one body—Jews or Greeks, slaves or free—and we were all made to drink of one Spirit.
> Indeed, the body does not consist of one member but of many. . . . Now you are the body of Christ and individually members of it. (1 Corinthians 12:12-14, 27)

Paul clearly applies this text to differing spiritual gifts, addressing one of the dividing issues in that community. But the image would apply equally well to other sources of division, such as that between Jews and Gentiles. Indeed, the Jerusalem Conference referred to in Acts 15 was an effort to define what unified the disciples of Jesus while allowing for appropriate diversity in matters like Old Testament rules on clean and unclean foods.

Another mark of God's vision for the church found in the New Testament is its inclusiveness. Christ's ministry was constantly crossing boundaries to reach those being left out. He ministered to lepers. He ate with tax collectors and notorious sinners. He spoke to women in public and associated with Samaritans. He told parables about lost sheep and lost coins and made it clear that, while Israel was special, the reign of God would include everyone. David Bosch, in his *Transforming Mission*, asks

> What is it that gave rise to the many sayings, parables, and stories that seem at the very least, to nourish the idea that, one day, God's covenant will reach far beyond the people of Israel? In my view there can be no doubt: the primary inspiration for all these stories could only have been the provocative, boundary-breaking nature of Jesus' own ministry.[6]

Hence, the decision to include Gentiles without first requiring them to convert to Judaism was the logical extension of Jesus' own ministry. The Holy Spirit led the church into a radical form of inclusiveness that was a powerful witness for God's redeeming love.

Taken as a whole, the New Testament is offering a vision of the church of Jesus Christ as embodying a visible unity while also characterized by diversity. Unity lies first and foremost in the confession that Jesus is Lord and in common worship of the risen Christ. While there is a common mission exemplified in evangelism and caring for the poor, differences in nationality, language, and spiritual gifts are expected and embraced. However, as the church lived its mission and worshiped the Lord, tensions arose. Sometimes they arose out of differences in nationality (Acts 6), doctrinal disputes (Acts 15, Galatians 3), and disagreements about missionary strategy (Acts 15:36-39). The church struggled to handle these tensions with love, grace, and unity while experiencing serious internal conflict.

From one point of view, this unity God wills for the church could be viewed as a commandment. We can think of it as something we ought to achieve, as if it were simply a matter of determining the proper course of action and then doing the right thing. But that violates the basic New Testament teaching that we are "saved by grace through faith" (Ephesians 2:8). Wesley talks about this in a helpful way. His principle is that the law and gospel are two ways of looking at the same relationship between God and humanity. He says,

> Yea, the very same words, considered in different respects, are parts both of the law and of the gospel. If they are considered as commandments, they are parts of the law: if as promises, of the gospel. Thus, "Thou shalt love the Lord thy God with all thy heart," when considered as a commandment, is a branch of the law; when regarded as a promise, is an essential part of the gospel—the gospel being no other than the commands of the law proposed by way of promises. Accordingly poverty of spirit, purity of heart, and whatever else is enjoined in the holy law of God, are no other, when viewed in a gospel light, than so many great and precious promises. . . .
>
> We may yet farther observe that every command in Holy Writ is only a covered promise.[7]

Thus, the unity of the Church (as well as its holiness, catholicity, and apostolicity) is a gift from God that is to be received rather than achieved.

Believing that unity is a gift changes our approach to it. First, we know it is God's will for God's people to be one. We then study and pray that God's "will be done on earth as it is in heaven." Second, we know that God is actively at working saving the world by grace. We then begin looking for signs of God at work, trusting that they exist and knowing that they might be obscured by the bad news that seems to frequently get more attention. Third, we then seek to align our lives, both in word and in deed, with what God is doing so that we can participate in God's saving, unifying activity. We are then able to live with confidence and hope in the future.

The Need of the World and a Christian Answer

The world needs a united Church. The peoples of the twenty-first century are characterized by interplay of complex interrelations and simultaneously increasing polarizations.

This is certainly true in economics. Under the rubric of globalization, a variety of changes have occurred since 1950. Manufacturing is now done on a global scale. Automobiles and airplanes are assembled in one country with parts made in a variety of countries. Manufacturers choose from many different locations all over the world for the best location to create their goods. Electronic communication means that many services such as call centers can be located in countries far away from the place where the service is delivered. Capital flows from all over the world, so that government debt in the form of bonds is financed by persons and institutions participating in a global market. The same is true for equities—not only do corporations operate internationally but their ownership is international as well. Increasingly, one can find goods and services from McDonald's restaurants to French clothing to Korean automobiles in many countries of the world.

At the same time, there are pressures for greater local control over economic realities and for people who value the specific traditions, ways of life, and products of their local culture. Indeed, part of globalization has been the search for different ways of doing things so that people from all over the world can experience the unique food or authentic practices of a particular region.

But the same trends of unity and diversity apply to politics as well. A number of problems such as global warming; terrorism; slavery; nuclear proliferation; genocide; diseases such as HIV/AIDS, avian flu, and malaria; and poverty can be addressed only by international cooperation. Yet, there are local pressures and realities that make each country's issues unique; and some countries are on the verge of breaking apart because different regions or ethnic groups have strong differences with others. In the field of education, we find universities emphasizing studies abroad and recruiting undergraduate and graduate students from a global pool of applicants. Global travel is now much easier than before. Instead of people reading about far-away countries, they are likely to vacation there in person. The ease of travel has fostered legal and illegal migration, so that in the United States there are an estimated twelve million illegal immigrants. Within developing countries like Mexico and China, internal migration causes pressures as well. In some metropolitan school districts in the United States, children will be speaking as many as three dozen languages.

In the midst of such major changes, what unifies a people? What holds a city together? What makes for a united country? What are the values that are so clearly held in common that living together is possible? How can appropriate freedoms be offered and guaranteed for diverse expressions? How do we keep from killing each other or oppressing each other or abusing each other? The world needs as many concrete expressions of diverse unity and reconciled diversity as possible. It needs a united Church. It does not need Christian churches dividing, splintering, or fracturing. If there was ever a time when the world needed to see how diversity can work within unity, it is now.

The Nature of the Church

In my view, the Christian church has a mission to proclaim peace on earth and God's loving offer of salvation. In the midst of a globalizing world, the mission of the Church is essential if the world is going to see both the deep values God intends for everyone as well as the need for diverse expressions of what it means to be fully human.

To fully accomplish its mission, the Church must be as united as possible with appropriate diversity. In many ways, the world's problems need the gospel. The peace proclaimed by the angels on the night of Christ's birth—the shalom or wholeness that comes from God—is precisely what the world needs to have. The Church must not only proclaim this gospel but embody it.

It is the nature of the Church to be the means of grace by which God's mission is accomplished. It worships God the Father; it is the body of God the Son; and God the Holy Spirit dwells in it with truth, love, and power. The Constitution of our United Methodist Church defines this clearly in its preamble:

> The church is a community of all true believers under the Lordship of Christ. It is the redeemed and redeeming fellowship in which the Word

of God is preached by persons divinely called, and the sacraments are duly administered according to Christ's own appointment. Under the discipline of the Holy Spirit the church seeks to provide for the maintenance of worship, the edification of believers, and the redemption of the world.

The church of Jesus Christ exists in and for the world, and its very dividedness is a hindrance to its mission in that world. (*The Book of Discipline of the United Methodist Church*, 2004, 21)

We are clear that the Triune God is the source, purpose, and power of all that the Church is and does. Just as there is one God, so there is one Church.

Yet this Church, because it is the body of Christ, shares in the two natures that characterized Jesus Christ. The Council of Chalcedon defined the doctrine of Christ's two natures: fully human and fully divine. In the same way, the Church is fully human and fully divine. On the one hand, it is composed of human beings and thus is a human institution. While Christ's full humanity was without sin, the Church is composed of sinners and thus is subject to the weaknesses and frailties of sinful humanity. It makes mistakes. It is sometimes short-sighted and self-centered. It sometimes misses obvious opportunities. It is possible to study the Church sociologically in the same way that scholars study other human institutions, and we can gain great insights from such analysis. All persons in the Church have experienced the human frailties, mistaken judgments, and sins that have led the Church to be less than what it should. Our human limitations in hearing God's directions and frequent unwillingness to follow those we clearly understand cause the Church to be less than fully obedient to the reign of God.

On the other hand, the Church is also divine. It is the Body of Christ whose Holy Spirit indwells it. In the Wesleyan tradition we would call the Church a means of grace—an ordinary channel through which God chooses to convey convincing, justifying, and sanctifying grace. Through the preaching of the Word of God and the administration of the sacraments, God uses the Church to convey grace to a needy world.

Most persons who have been active participants in the Church can also testify that they have seen it do amazing acts of love, evangelism, and sacrificial service to the world. People have experienced God in countless ways through the preaching, worship, Bible study, and social justice ministries of God's Church.

Many varied stories can be told. But the one that sticks in my mind is the Sunday I preached a terrible sermon. I felt like it was the worst sermon ever delivered in the history of Christianity. Despite my hard work of preparation, it just fell flat. As I walked down the aisle, exiting during the last hymn, I thought to myself, "It is a good thing these are Christian people. Otherwise they would be asking the bishop to move me immediately." That Sunday two different persons greeted me outside the sanctuary to tell me that something special had happened during worship. One said, "Preacher, your sermon touched me deeply. You must have had a microphone over my breakfast table. Thanks for giving me exactly what I needed to hear." That's when I was reminded again that God was actually present in worship and using my feeble words to accomplish amazing things. We know that Christ truly is present wherever "two or more are gathered in his name" (Matthew 18:20).

The Mission of the Church

Where Christ is present, the Church is energized to participate in God's mission of saving the world. God is a missionary God, and the Bible is a missionary book. To accomplish God's purposes, God the Father sent the Son to be born as a baby in Bethlehem "for us and for our salvation."[8] In order to accomplish that mission, Christ lived, taught, died, and was resurrected on the third day. He had gathered disciples, and on Pentecost the third person of the Trinity descended and formed those disciples into a Church.

Many theologians today closely tie together the basic nature of the church and its missionary nature.[9] Carlos Cardoza-Orlandi quotes Emil Brunner as saying, "Mission is to the church what combustion is to fire," and draws the conclusion that "there is no church without mission."[10] Too many congregations in the United States, including United

Methodist congregations, have lost their sense of mission. They are internally focused and consistently ask how they can better care for those who are already members. They have become more of a club than a church. To be a church is to participate in God's mission of saving the world. That requires an outward focus and a willingness to sacrifice for the cause of Christ. We need to do whatever it takes to allow the Holy Spirit to use the Church to accomplish God's purposes.

For more than one hundred years, leaders of the ecumenical movement have quoted Jesus' words in John 17:21, "that they may all be one . . . so that the world may believe," as a primary authorization for linking together the unity of the church and mission and evangelism. Consider a conversation between a United Methodist evangelist and someone who is not part of the Church. The evangelist makes the offer for the person to believe in God and find salvation, including participation in the life of a congregation.[11] She speaks movingly about God's love for all humanity and invites her friend to join a community where the peace of Christ and the love of God and the redeeming power of the Holy Spirit are evident in their lives and their relationships. Perhaps the friend comes from a dysfunctional family where conflict and hatred occur more frequently than togetherness and caring. But then the prospective convert asks, "Why are you Christians always separating from each other and arguing?" The lack of unity among Christians is a stumbling block to authentic evangelism. In his sermon on "The General Spread of the Gospel" John Wesley named "the lives of Christians" as "the grand stumbling block," which God needs to remove in order to accomplish God's purposes.

The Pilgrim Way of the Church

Yet, no evangelist can tell a prospective Christian that the Church is perfect. God has chosen to use limited, sinful human beings to accomplish God's purposes, and yet has promised God's abiding presence and power to ensure its ultimate success. We are in many ways a people on a journey of faith under the guidance of the Holy Spirit. A recent statement of the dialogue commission of World Methodist Council and Roman Catholic Church aptly summarizes this journey of the church:

> Unity, holiness, catholicity and apostolicity are already gifts of God to his Church, marks of God's continuing and faithful presence. But we are a pilgrim people, and those marks are both gifts and goals, already present but not yet fully realised. As we seek to place ourselves and our communities at the service of the divine mission, we seek also by God's grace to grow towards entire sanctification: "Just as the Church longs for the oneness of its members in love and prays for it in its liturgy, so it waits in hope for spiritual gifts that will lead it to a higher level of holiness, a more evident fullness of catholicity, and a greater fidelity in apostolicity. This striving after perfection in the God-given marks of the Church implies an ecumenical imperative. All Christian churches should pray and work toward an eventual restoration of organic unity."[12]

We say in the Nicene Creed that the church is one, holy, catholic, and apostolic, and yet know that we are still living into God's gifts to us in each of these aspects. In a deep sense, we have been given the gift of unity already. But we know that we have only partially accepted that unity and we are still living into it. In the same way, the church has been gifted with holiness, catholicity, and apostolicity. Yet, each of them is really present, though not fully. While individuals are going on toward entire sanctification, so is God's church. God has not perfected it yet.

Sometimes we fail to see these spiritual realities because our eyes are accustomed to other things. Almost every time I preach I offer the following prayer: "God, thank you for your presence in this place. We trust your promise that where two or three are gathered in your name, you will be there too. Yet, sometimes we don't get it. So we ask, open our eyes that we might see you. Open our ears that we might hear your word. Then give us hands and feet that we might be doers of the word and not hearers only." It is a matter of faith—while acknowledging our sinfulness, we believe that God is at work in our midst, leading the Church toward fulfilling its purpose and attaining its intended reality.

In a way, this is the Stockdale paradox referred to in Jim Collins's *Good to Great*. Named for Admiral Jim Stockdale, the highest ranking prisoner of war held in the "Hanoi Hilton" during the Vietnam War, the paradox pays tribute to his ability to survive a brutal prison for eight years. He told Collins that the optimists died in prison of broken hearts. Instead, Collins learned that the secret of survival was to "retain faith that you will prevail in the end, regardless of the difficulties, and at the same time confront the most brutal facts of your current reality, whatever they might be."[13] Understood theologically, this same point can be stated as believing that God will get us through and lead us to final victory, while acknowledging that we are wandering in the wilderness at the present time and that the promised land is a long way off.

Historical Context

There is a larger context for our discussions of unity. The discussion that follows is a broad overview, which needs more careful and nuanced interpretation; but it may be helpful for understanding the current issues. The early church showed tensions even during New Testament times. Paul's first letter to the Corinthians is evidence that even within that community there were divisive issues. Over time, tensions developed over the doctrine of God, over language (Greek or Latin), and over the role of bishops. Some separations took place, particularly after Christianity was tolerated and then received official status in the Roman Empire.

However, the first major split came in 1054 when the Eastern church and those in communion with the Bishop of Rome separated and condemned each other. Further splits within the Western church came with the Protestant Reformation, as people in Europe moved into a variety of different churches in the sixteenth and seventeenth centuries. Broadly speaking, Europe saw the emergence of Lutheran, Reformed, Anabaptist, and Anglican churches. The English Civil War and the wars of religion on the European continent in the seventeenth century further changed the shape of religion there. In response to the conflict, the English developed a new concept: toleration of different churches within the same political unit. These came to be known as denominations, and the Act of Toleration in 1689 was a milestone in providing partial religious freedom.

The formation of the United States and the passage of the Bill of Rights as amendments to the Constitution ensured that America would provide a new pattern of Christian church practice. The number of churches multiplied greatly during the first hundred years of the American experiment in religious freedom.

Beginning in the late 1800s a number of factors led Protestants to begin seeking closer relationships and eventual unity. Chief among these factors was the need to evangelize persons in Europe and America and the realities of mission work in Africa, Asia, and South America. Many count the missionary conference held in Edinburgh, Scotland, in 1910 as a key step forward in the modern ecumenical movement. Formation of the World Methodist Council, various national councils of Churches, the World Council of Churches and many independent interdenominational or parachurch bodies were supplemented by the teachings of Vatican II. Many thought that the ecumenical movement had great momentum and promise, and they looked forward to a day when all Christians would be united in one visible church.

Within the Methodist branch of the church, three denominations moved first toward closer cooperation and then toward merger. In 1939, the Methodist Episcopal Church; the Methodist Episcopal Church, South; and the Methodist Protestant Church united to form The Methodist Church. The Evangelical Association and the United Brethren in Christ joined together in 1946, and the Evangelical United Brethren and Methodists merged in 1968 to form The United Methodist Church. The Commission on Pan-Methodist Union has been working to bring closer relations between The United Methodist Church and the African Methodist Episcopal; African Methodist Episcopal, Zion; and Christian Methodist Episcopal Churches.

Thus, one might summarize the period of 1500–1900 as a time for division within Christianity and the period since then as a time for greater unity. Many ecumenically minded persons no longer hold a goal of organic unity, but instead seek mutual recognition of membership and ministry. Many churches are seeking full communion that would allow for Eucharistic sharing and common mission. The United Methodist Church makes two clear statements about unity in its constitution. In the Preamble it says, "The church of Jesus Christ exists in and for the world, and its very dividedness is a hindrance to its mission in that world" (*Book of Discipline*, 21). Article VI of Division I elaborates:

> *Ecumenical Relations*—As part of the church universal, The United Methodist Church believes that the Lord of the church is calling Christians everywhere to strive toward unity; and therefore it will seek, and work for, unity at all levels of church life: through world relationships with other Methodist churches and united churches related to The Methodist Church or The Evangelical United Brethren Church, through councils of churches, and through plans of union and covenantal relationships with churches of Methodist or other denominational traditions. (*Book of Discipline*, ¶6)

A deep commitment to Christian unity has been in the blood of United Methodists for a long time. This deep value, developed over years of tradition going back to Wesley's efforts in the eighteenth century, has been an important characteristic of our witness and ministry. The idea of "amicable separation" discussed before and during the 2004 General Conference thus shocked many and violated their sense of what should happen. Yet, the stresses and strains on our internal unity have increased in the last several decades, and it is crucial that we pay more attention to what holds us together. Many have taken our unity for granted and now need to think more clearly about why separation is a bad idea.

Necessary Elements of Unity

For United Methodists, a useful starting point comes in the opening paragraph of John Wesley's "Thoughts upon Methodism" written in 1786. He wrote,

> I am not afraid that the people called Methodists should ever cease to exist either in Europe or America. But I am afraid, lest they should only exist as a dead sect, having the form of religion without the power. And this undoubtedly will be the case, unless they hold fast both the doctrine, spirit, and discipline with which they first set out.[14]

Note the three elements here—doctrine, spirit, and discipline. If we understand that by "spirit" Wesley was referring to the way in which God was using the Methodists to accomplish God's purposes, then those three can become basic categories for discussing essential elements of Christian unity: mission, discipline, and doctrine.

Mission

For decades, United Methodism and its predecessor denominations could take many things for granted. Most people in this country were at least nominally Christian, and we knew the basics of our doctrine and knew what our mission was. The 1960s and 1970s were a turbulent time. The culture changed and no longer supported Christianity. Our Church was challenged. In the adaptation to the challenges, our best leaders were preoccupied with institutional maintenance due to the merger of the Methodist and Evangelical United Brethren churches. We presumed that our cultural dominance would continue forever. But as the world changed, the Church became more and more irrelevant. Some of our leaders who sought relevance abandoned the basics of the faith, and the Church was set adrift.

United Methodism lives by its mission. We were not founded in a doctrinal dispute. Wesley repeatedly said his teachings were the teachings of the Church of England; and Otterbein, Boehm, and Albright would have concurred. Our origins lie with the effort to carry the gospel to the poor, the unchurched, and the immigrant. When we are clear about our mission, we thrive. When we are confused about our mission or when we adopt a partial mission in place of the whole gospel, we die. One church I know, when asked what their mission was, answered "We keep the building open for weddings and funerals, and help student pastors to go be real ministers elsewhere." Another congregation, when asked what was the difference between them and the Rotary Club, could not think of any difference.[15] Also, when evangelists focus on saving souls like spiritual scalps on their belts, neglecting justice, and when social justice activists fail to name Jesus and invite personal commitments of lives to Christ as Lord and Savior, our mission is poorly conceived and poorly lived. We are prepared to evaluate our congregation's life by what it provides me and my family, and allow all of our neighbors to go to hell or to live in an earthly hell while we make no response.

The deep and abiding problem of many Protestant congregations in the United States is that they have ceased to be missionary outposts to reach the unchurched for the reign of God. Instead, too often they are clubs existing for the benefit of their members. In a club-type congregation, it is important that "membership has its privileges." That is the significance of paragraphs 120-22 in the *Book of Discipline, 2004*. The General Conference adopted the single sentence, "The mission of the Church is to make disciples of Jesus Christ," but it also added the second sentence, "Local churches provide the most significant arena through which disciple-making occurs" (*Book of Discipline*, ¶120). Too often our United Methodist connection was conceived by many as a hierarchy where local congregations sent money for real mission work elsewhere. This mission statement turns that concept upside down. Local congregations are now seen as the main arena for accomplishing our mission. The general agencies, annual conferences, and districts exist primarily to assist local congregations in their mission. That includes connecting them for the support of missionaries, seminaries, colleges, hospitals, and social justice ministries that no one congregation could do on its own.

Further, the *Discipline* outlines a holistic process of making disciples. It includes outreach, evangelism, worship, Sunday school, Bible study, and social justice activities. It says,

> The Process for Carrying Out Our Mission—We make disciples as we:
> —proclaim the gospel, seek, welcome and gather persons into the body of Christ;
> —lead persons to commit their lives to God through baptism by water and the spirit and profession of faith in Jesus Christ;
> —nurture persons in Christian living through worship, the sacraments, spiritual disciplines, and other means of grace, such as Wesley's Christian conferencing;

—send persons into the world to live lovingly and justly as servants of Christ by healing the sick, feeding the hungry, caring for the stranger, freeing the oppressed, being and becoming a compassionate, caring presence, and working to develop social structures that are consistent with the gospel; and

—continue the mission of seeking, welcoming, and gathering persons into the community of the body of Christ. (*Book of Discipline*, ¶122)

For more than one hundred years too many clergy and laity in the UMC have separated evangelism and social justice.

The problem here is that too many people do not understand what is meant by disciple-making. They read paragraph 120 and go no farther. This leads to misunderstandings. To "make disciples of Jesus Christ" is to refer to the Great Commission in Matthew 28. It summarizes the whole gospel of Matthew. But that means disciple-making includes Matthew 25—the parable of the sheep and goats. It includes Matthew 22 and the Great Commandments. It includes the Sermon on the Mount. Without understanding the entire gospel, too often disciple-making fails to embody God's complete mission for the Church.

One component of our unity is to focus on our mission. John 17:21 gives the purpose of unity as being "that the world may believe." The kind of mission work that will truly evangelize the world will be diverse; it has to be. God, in God's wisdom, has made us red, brown, yellow, black, and white. We are old and young. Some of us like hip-hop and others prefer country music. For me personally, the third movement of Beethoven's Ninth Symphony is in stiff competition with Handel's *Messiah* as the best music of all time. But I am well aware that my preference for dead-German music will not reach many persons in the United States today, let alone millions in Europe, Africa, and Asia.

There may have been a time when the assumption was that all Methodist clergy could serve any Methodist church. I believe that was gone by 1850, when there were evident tensions between city Methodists and rural Methodists. But today, in making appointments of clergy to churches, bishops need a variety of persons in the conference so that their abilities to relate to the different subcultures of each conference mean that all of our churches receive the clergy leadership they need. Western Kansas is different from eastern Kansas, and our rural areas are not the same as the suburbs of Wichita and Kansas City. If all the clergy in the United Methodist Church were alike, our missionary impact would be crippled.

Thus, our unity must have diversity. Some of the people with whom I disagree about many things are better situated to do evangelism in their context than I am. They may be doing it in a way that doesn't quite fit my view of how to do church, but we need all kinds of missionaries to reach all kinds of people. We need Yankees as well as Texans; we need seminary-educated persons as well as part-time local pastors. We need women and men, African-Americans, Asians, Native Americans, Hispanic/Latinos/Latinas, and Anglo folk. When you look around the United States today, we have people from all the continents, except Antarctica, coming here; and we need missionaries in this country who can culturally adapt the gospel to reach them. There are people doing things with skateboard ministry to young people with orange hair, body piercing, and tattoos; I praise God for them. I am not one of them, but I can envision a church big enough to include lots of different kinds of people. We have our model of that in Paul, who in 1 Corinthians 9:22 said "I have become all things to all people, that I might by all means save some." Liberals need conservatives and conservatives need liberals. If one group leaves, we are all worse off.

Too many of our congregations are fully prepared to do mission and effective ministry if the 1950s ever come back. Some of them are perfectly orthodox in doctrine, but they are spiritually dead. **I will argue long and hard for the extreme center, but I am totally opposed to the dead center.** No matter how orthodox your congregation is, if the people are not filled with Christ's love, if they don't have a passion for souls, if they are not willing to cross cultural bridges to reach new groups of people, they are not being faithful. We do not need just one embodiment of the gospel.

Ecclesiology

This leads to the question of ecclesiology. Like most Protestants, and especially American Protestants, we have a poorly formed doctrine of the Church. Article V of the Confession of Faith says,

We believe the Christian Church is the community of all true believers
under the Lordship of Christ. We believe it is one, holy, apostolic and
catholic. It is the redemptive fellowship in which the Word of God is
preached by men divinely called, and the sacraments are duly administered according to Christ's own appointment. Under the discipline of
the Holy Spirit the Church exists for the maintenance of worship, the
edification of believers and the redemption of the world. (*Book of
Discipline*, 67)

This article focuses on preaching the Word of God, administering the
sacraments, discipline under the Holy Spirit and the mission of worship,
making disciples of believers, and participating in God's mission of saving
the world.

However, it allows for at least two different versions. Some could read this
text as a narrowly defined group of persons who all think alike. Such a
church would make uniformity a goal, and the least disagreement would
require separation. Such a group would not tolerate dissension and would
squash any innovations. Sadly, there are such churches in the United States.

The other alternative is the playing-field concept where there is a
spacious area for people to take up different interpretations. The people
of God are a big enough group that inevitably there will be many different positions all within the boundaries of the playing field. Some will
be on the left side and others on the right. Some will be low and others
will be high. Some will stand in the extreme center of the field; others
unfortunately will be in the dead center. What I like about this
metaphor is, first, that it respects the various contributions that each
group or person makes to the whole. A living, dynamic body of believers needs that kind of tension and lively interchange in order to keep
its missionary action effective. At the same time, this metaphor names
the existence of boundaries. There are defining limits to the Church
beyond which one can be said to have left the denomination. Violation
of our doctrinal standards and violation of our discipline are both ways
of leaving. There are some among us who hate any mention of boundaries and argue that such a vision is oppressive. I say that Scripture and
tradition, not to mention the modern science of organizational behavior, insist that we set limits and enforce them.

But the most crucial way of delineating our boundary, our unity, is to say that we are a missionary organization. In the *Circuit Rider* edition on evangelism a few years ago, Kevin Ruffcorn's article was entitled "If It Ain't Heaven, It's a Mission Field." His argument is that every congregation is located on the mission field. When my great-aunt wanted to be a missionary, she wrote the Board of Missions from her home in Iowa and volunteered. Everyone knew that America was a Christian country, and mission work happened overseas. So she volunteered and was sent to China. If America ever was a Christian nation (and it is a very doubtful claim), we are so no longer. All American Christians live on the mission field.

It is our common mission of making disciples of Jesus Christ that unites us. We will do it in different ways. We do not always understand what a disciple is or what evangelism is. But we are doing it, and we know it when we see it. When General Conference passed the mission statement in 1996, some believed that living into that statement would take twenty years. We are moving more quickly than they ever dreamed possible. The mission statement is now more deeply engrained in our ethos than I ever imagined it would be, and I am grateful to the Holy Spirit for using that to help transform our denomination.

Discipline

Several times John Wesley quoted a phrase he said was from the early church: "The soul and the body make a man; the spirit and discipline make a Christian"; "implying," he said, "that none could be real Christians without the help of Christian discipline."[16] United Methodists know that discipline is essential to salvation and to effective ministry. One of the book titles I like best is Charles Ferguson's *Organizing to Beat the Devil: Methodists and the Making of America*. We know how to organize. But when you have forgotten that your mission is to beat the devil, the organization becomes an end in itself.

Hence, some people have been led by the Spirit to a strong missionary outreach that does new things for the Lord. Unfortunately, they too often make the mistake of neglecting discipline. When discipline is devalued, eventually a new ministry withers and dies.

We need to understand the ways in which our connectional system embodies the biblical values of unity and diversity in pursuit of our mission to make disciples of Jesus Christ. We need to embody spiritual values in all that we do. Our conferences need to be means of grace and times of conferring about what to teach, how to teach, and what to do. We have an itinerant system of deploying preachers because we believe it is the best way to accomplish our mission. I believe God works through the appointment process. I believed that when I was a pastor. I believed that when I was a seminary professor. As a bishop of the Church, I still believe it even though I am humbled by it. Itineracy, connectionalism, and other aspects of our discipline are sometimes the objects of complaint by those who misunderstand them and even by those who understand them fully, or in response to leaders who failed to act in Christlike ways. Leaders of the church—bishops, clergy, general agencies, lay leaders, all of us who lead—must faithfully guard the Church's discipline for the sake of its mission. We have to improve the quality of the covenant relationship among the clergy in conference and between the clergy and their bishops. We must strengthen the accountability of bishops to each other and to their conferences and to the Church. We need to improve the accountability of our general agencies to the Church and the accountability of local congregations to our discipline. We need to empower laity for ministry. We must support clergy when they need to be prophetic to local churches.

Such accountability requires a special role for bishops. I believe that we have an obligation to uphold the *Book of Discipline*, and to do so in a way that highlights its spiritual and missional purposes. However, we cannot do it alone. Bishops are constrained by the ways in which the *Discipline* is written, and there are important roles played by the clergy session and the full session of annual conferences. We all have a role in increasing our collective accountability to one another and thereby to Christ.

We live in a time of disconnection in American culture. Robert Putnam's *Bowling Alone* helps us understand why forming community—

what he calls social capital—is so hard today. It has made all kinds of community much more difficult than they were fifty years ago, and not just for us, but for every organization in the United States. In such an environment, leadership is very difficult and requires extraordinary effort. We need to raise up a new generation of Christian leaders who are intelligent, passionate, visionary, politically savvy, and theologically astute— leaders who can guide our Church into its preferred future. That includes clergy, laity, General Conference delegates, and bishops. How we raise up those persons, mentor them, and then select them is critically important.

Discipline is also part of the Christian life for individuals. The General Rules are meant to apply to every United Methodist:

> It is therefore expected of all who continue therein that they should continue to evidence their desire of salvation, *First:* by doing no harm . . . *Secondly:* By doing good . . . *Thirdly:* By attending upon all the ordinances of God. (*Book of Discipline*, 72-74)

When persons join our denomination, we ask that they commit to "faithfully participate in its ministries by your prayers, your presence, your gifts, and your service."[17] When these rules are actualized in some United Methodist congregations, they talk about the expectations. One of the best set of these was in place when I was appointed pastor of Stonebridge UMC in McKinney, Texas. They made it clear that membership has no privileges. Anyone can participate in the ministries of the Church whether they are members or not. But membership was a significant step in one's spiritual journey that, if properly followed, would bring each person closer to Christ. Members were expected to be in worship every week, to be part of a small group where they were spiritually fed, and to be part of a small group where they fed others. They called this "Church plus two." In addition, members were expected to tithe or move toward tithing.

The theological underpinning of spiritual disciplines is that we are saved by grace through faith. Thus, as we participate in the means of grace, we find God's grace transforming our lives and empowering us to transform our communities. Thus, Christian disciples are practicing the disciplines that shape them. In addition to prayer, fasting, worship, and the other ordinances of God listed in the General Rules, we know that there are new disciplines such as walking a labyrinth, retreats, compassion for the poor, and works of mercy that are spiritual disciplines as well. As John Wesley said (and our doctrinal standards teach), these spiritual disciplines are the ordinary channels through which God is saving us.

Doctrine

The changes in American culture that came in the 1960s and 1970s were multifaceted and included not only turmoil over social issues but also changes in technology, science, and theology. Part of that was the rise of mass culture transmitted through movies, television, and now the Internet. When they were young, my children could name all four Mutant Ninja Turtles—Raphael, Michelangelo, Donatello, and Leonardo—before they could name any of the twelve disciples. Perhaps I was a bad parent. But the reality is that most of our children were more deeply influenced by these kinds of characters than by Bible stories.

We can no longer assume we live in a Christian culture that will teach people the faith. For years the main question in many parts of our country was, "Which church do you attend?" People knew the answer to that even if they didn't attend church—they knew which church they would attend if they ever did attend church. Now, in many parts of our country the question is "Are you a Christian?" There are more Muslims in the United States than Episcopalians. One of my college friends was raised Methodist, then United Methodist, and while in college became first Hare Krishna, then Sufi (a version of mystical Islam), and then a Pentecostal speaking-in-tongues Christian. The world we live in is a marketplace of ideas and religious options. It is more like the first-century Roman Empire than nineteenth-century America. One key difference is that we are moving toward a culture that is post-Christian, where people believe Christianity has been tried and found wanting.

FOUR LEVELS OF DOCTRINE

While this transition was going on, our Church was de-emphasizing scriptural authority and the basic doctrinal standards that had guided us for so long. Part of my work as a scholar was to argue for a particular understanding of what constitutes United Methodist doctrine. I believe we have four levels. At the highest level is Scripture. We are a Bible-believing church. But the Bible alone is not sufficient. During the last 2000 years of God's great missionary effort to save the world through his Church, we have had to develop doctrine precisely to be faithful to Scripture.

For example, the doctrine of the Trinity is a biblical doctrine. It is a way of reading the whole Scripture that is consistent with its overall message. But it took the church almost three hundred years to get it right. The Nicene Creed was our way of saying "This is the true Christian faith, and not this." To say that Jesus Christ is "true God from true God, of one substance with the Father" is not quoting Scripture. Over the last two thousand years our doctrine has developed and expanded to cope with new missionary settings, always seeking to be faithful to God's self-revelation in Christ as witnessed by the apostles and recorded in the Scriptures. So it is that doctrinal development is normal, and it is usually messy. We human beings are sinful, often self-centered and narrow-minded, and so we argue about how best to give faithful witness to Christ in our particular context. But we need doctrinal standards in order to be faithful to the original "faith that was once for all entrusted to the saints" (Jude 3).

There are two other crucial elements here. First, we need to teach the Bible. Somehow in our congregations we have allowed our people to grow up Christian without knowing the Bible. I am a fourth-generation Methodist and then United Methodist. It was only in seminary that I finally learned the Bible, and even there I was just given the tools to start learning. Much of my biblical knowledge came from my preaching ministry over the years. One of the problems our seminaries face is we are sending them men and women who are called to preach, but they are not formed by Scripture and tradition, and they lack basic knowledge that one could have presumed in earlier days.

Second, we need to develop and inculcate our Wesleyan way of reading the text. Doctrine is based on a particular construal of the wholeness of Scripture. On September 11, 2001, I was teaching at Cliff College in England. I started my lectures on the theology of evangelism by claiming that the most important biblical text in understanding God is 1 John 4:8, "God is love." I thought this was noncontroversial and obvious. I was stopped by a student who said, "No, the most important of God's attributes is God's sovereignty." There you had it. In John Wesley's home country the ancient controversy between Arminians and Calvinists being played out again. But its battle ground was how you read Scripture.

John Wesley's conception of Scripture says in his comment on Romans 12:6 that biblical interpretation should be according to the analogy of faith, that is, "according to the general tenor of [the Scriptures]; according to that grand scheme of doctrine which is delivered therein, touching original sin, justification by faith, and present, inward salvation."[18]

This helps explain the deep structure of DISCIPLE Bible Study, which I believe to be one of the greatest contributions to The United Methodist Church in my lifetime. When you see key words like "sin," "justified," and "sanctified" in the headings, you realize that the authors are teaching a United Methodist way of reading the text. We trust the Bible, and we have a distinctive way of reading it, which informs our doctrine.

The second level of doctrine is made up of our constitutionally protected standards of doctrine—Articles of Religion, Confession of Faith, General Rules, Wesley's Sermons, and Wesley's New Testament Notes. These are the primary means by which we interpret Scripture. They are difficult to change; and hence, they have shaped the Methodist movement, the Evangelical Association, and the United Brethren in Christ for centuries. All other doctrinal statements, whether it is part II of the *Book of Discipline*, the Social Principles, or Council of Bishops teaching documents, are to be measured against Scripture and the doctrinal standards.

But this means we need a much greater working knowledge of what they teach and how to apply them. Notice I named five. How many United Methodists could even get that far? Even the clergy? How many of them have a working knowledge of all five and use them in their preaching and teaching? Not enough.

When I was working on my honors thesis in philosophy at the University of Kansas, my advisor, a practicing Presbyterian, said, "You're a Methodist. You must believe in the warmed heart." I had no idea what he meant. When I got to Perkins School of Theology as a seminary student, my second semester I enrolled in Albert Outler's course "Wesley and the Wesleyan Tradition." Listening to Albert lecture that spring was like Roberta Flack's song; he was "Telling my whole life with his words, Killing me softly with his song." It is like T. S. Eliot's poem that says,

> We shall not cease from exploration
> And the end of all our exploring
> Will be to arrive where we started
> And know the place for the first time.[19]

I came to understand that Wesley was capable of telling me who I was and where I needed to go. After years of preaching, I am more convinced of this than ever. What a joy it is to find that not only is Wesley a wise theological friend and mentor but his Sermons and Notes are our church's doctrinal standards whose content I have promised to preach and maintain.

The third level of doctrine is made up of contemporary statements of the General Conference in the *Book of Discipline*, Social Principles, and Resolutions that are by their nature more variable. They can change every time the General Conference meets. We are not very clear about what levels of authority each of these has, but none of them can be allowed to violate the doctrinal standards. Fourth, there is a sense in which our liturgy and hymnody are official doctrine. We are not at all clear about what force they should have, but it is clear that they shape the lives and beliefs of our communities more powerfully than do the doctrinal standards.

This is the deep structure of our doctrine, and it is not widely understood. We need better doctrinal competence among our Church's leaders. When bishops ordain elders each spring, we ask them, "Have you studied the doctrines of The United Methodist Church? After full examination do you believe that our doctrines are in harmony with the Holy Scriptures? Will you preach and maintain them?" (*Book of Discipline*, ¶336). Bishops ask these questions because persons called to the ministry of an elder are not called to preach their own theology. They are called to preach and maintain the faith of the Church expressed in its official doctrines. That is the reason that teaching things contrary to our standards of doctrine is a chargeable offense. (*Book of Discipline*, ¶¶2707.1 ff.)

DOCTRINE AND OUR CHRISTIAN WORLDVIEW

Doctrine shapes the spiritual world in which we live. John Wesley's way of putting this same point comes in a letter to Conyers Middleton, speaking of how doctrine has a spiritual purpose:

> The Second point to be considered is, what is real, genuine Christianity? whether we speak of it as a principle in the soul, or as a scheme or system of doctrine. Christianity, taken in the latter sense, is that system of doctrine which describes the character above recited, which promises, it shall be mine, (provided I will not rest till I attain,) and which tells me how I may attain it.[20]

Consider for a minute the fact that our inattention to doctrine and our lack of interest in evangelism are deeply intertwined. We sometimes don't practice evangelism because we have theological commitments that lean toward universal salvation. If you believe that all persons will be saved eventually, there is less urgency to offer a saving relationship with Christ now. When you don't believe it matters if you are a Christian, then why invite someone to become one? If being a Christian is a once-saved-always-saved phenomenon, then it is OK to claim you are a Christian and never darken the doorway of a congregation. John Wesley said there is no such thing as solitary Christianity, and we need a richer and fuller description of Christian discipleship with higher expectations than we have been used to giving.

Yet, we have to be careful about the role of doctrine. Brian McLaren's recent book *Generous Orthodoxy* revives a term coined by Hans Frei, who said, "Generosity without orthodoxy is nothing, but orthodoxy without generosity is worse than nothing."[21] This is the point behind John Wesley's statement in the sermon "The Way to the Kingdom." He says,

> For neither does religion consist in *orthodoxy*, or *right opinions*; which, although they are not properly outward things, are not in the heart, but the understanding. A man may be orthodox in every point; he may not only espouse right opinions, but zealously defend them against all opposers; he may think justly concerning the incarnation of our Lord, concerning the ever blessed Trinity, and every other doctrine contained in the oracles of God. He may assent to all the three creeds—that called the Apostles', the Nicene, and the Athanasian—and yet 'tis possible he may have no religion at all, no more than a Jew, Turk, or pagan. He may be almost as orthodox as the devil (though indeed not altogether; for every man errs in something, whereas we can't well conceive him to hold any erroneous opinion) and may all the while be as great a stranger as he to the religion of the heart.[22]

Wesley knew too many people who could speak well about religion, but they weren't living it out. It is all about love of God and love of neighbor. We can be absolutely right; but if we have not love, we are nothing. 1 Corinthians 13 provides important guidance here.

Yet, Wesley was living in a culture where the basics of the faith could be taken for granted. Despite the threat of deism, the cultural power of Christianity in the 1700s was immense. His problem was how to get nominal Christians to become real Christians. We live in a different time where the very churches themselves are in danger of becoming secularized. I have been in too many congregations where there was no mention of Jesus, no offer of salvation, and no clear challenge to the secular, anti-Christian messages influencing persons' lives. When we don't pay attention to the doctrinal basis for a Christian worldview, many other efforts fail.

For example, take the sin of racism. It is a huge issue still facing the United States, and getting more complicated as more immigrants from more countries make a home among us. Our church has stood strongly alongside the immigrant in our teaching. But our witness against racism depends directly upon an understanding that God created all people in God's own image, regardless of skin color, language, ethnicity, or whatever. All persons are precious in God's sight. The fight against racism is a doctrinal issue that rests ultimately on our doctrine of God and of creation. It rests on our understanding that God is a God of love who risked all, even becoming human for our salvation.

These are the ten essential doctrines that tie us together in very deep ways:

Trinity, including Christology
Creation
Sin
Repentance
Justification
New Birth
Assurance
Sanctification
Grace
Mission[23]

The case that these are the essential doctrines could be made from an analysis of The United Methodist Church's official standards of doctrine. Reading the Articles of Religion and Confession of Faith along with Wesley's sermons and Notes could provide the basis for the claim that our essential doctrines are related to the Triune God and the way of salvation. But there is a more inductive way to show the importance of these ten. They answer the three most important questions of religion:

1. Who is God?
2. What must we do to be saved, that is in a right relationship with God?
3. What is the way of salvation?

The Nicene Creed specifies who is God. There is one God in three persons, Father, Son, and Holy Spirit. This God became incarnate in Jesus of Nazareth who lived, died, and rose again for us and for our salvation.

Christ Jesus is fully human and fully divine, and by his death we have been offered salvation. We are saved by grace through faith for good works (Ephesians 2:8-10). The Church is God's chief means of grace, which God uses to accomplish God's mission of saving every human being and the whole creation.

Diversity in Unity: Catholic Spirit

Within that outline of who God is, what salvation is, and the grace by which we receive it and live it out, there is plenty of room for significant disagreements. For the Church, there is an ongoing tension between its unity and its diversity. Both are part of God's intention and both are attested in Scripture, and yet there has been ongoing controversy since apostolic times about what each means and how to discern the best pattern for each.

On the one hand, the unity of the Church is God's intention. We have already discussed that above. Ephesians 4:4-6 says it succinctly:

> There is one body and one Spirit, just as you were called to the one hope of your calling, one Lord, one faith, one baptism, one God and Father of all, who is above all and through all and in all.

If the one God is using the Church as a means of grace, calling all of humanity to peace and love, then part of the Church's witness should be the visible display of that peace and love within its life as an institution and among its various members individually.

Functionally speaking, the unity of the Church also provides coherent answers to the largest questions human beings ask. It is the answer about ultimate meaning and ultimate reality. For evangelistic and apologetic purposes, we need to be able to point to the same reality with a description that is basically the same for all Christians. This is the purpose of the Nicene and Apostles' Creeds. However, given the increasingly multireligious environment in many countries of the world, the Apostles' Creed is not as useful. It is possible to read that creed as teaching three gods. I believe a member of the Church of Jesus Christ of Latter-day Saints (commonly known as Mormons) could recite the Apostles' Creed with integrity. Mormon doctrine does not agree with the Nicene Creed, and thus they are not Christians.

At the same time, God intends diversity. On the day of Pentecost, the Holy Spirit spoke through Peter so that every one heard in their own language. We have intentionally translated the Bible into different languages ever since that day. We have seen that the eschatological vision of the New Testament is that one day

> at the name of Jesus
>> every knee should bend,
>> in heaven and on earth and under the earth,
> and every tongue should confess
>> that Jesus Christ is Lord,
>> to the glory of God the Father. (Philippians 2:10-11)

Inevitably this means that the Church of Jesus Christ will include people from all nations, all races, all language groups, and all ethnic groups. Thus, how we hold fast both the unity and diversity which God intends is an important part of being the Church.

John Wesley's important sermon "Catholic Spirit" gives us significant help on this point. He begins with the claim, "It is allowed even by those who do not pay this great debt that love is due to all mankind, the royal law, 'Thou shalt love thy neighbour as thyself,' carrying its own evidence to all that hear it." He then argues that Christians have an even stronger motivation for loving their neighbors, citing Jesus' command to love even our enemies. He then asks,

> All men approve of this. But do all men practise it? Daily experience shows the contrary. Where are even the Christians who 'love one another, as he hath given us commandment'? How many hindrances lie in the way! The two grand, general hindrances are, first, that they can't all think alike; and in consequence of this, secondly, they can't all walk alike; but in several smaller points their practice must differ in proportion to the difference of their sentiments.

But although a difference in opinions or modes of worship may prevent an entire external union, yet need it prevent our union in affection? Though we can't think alike, may we not love alike? May we not be of one heart, though we are not of one opinion? Without all doubt we may. Herein all the children of God may unite, notwithstanding these smaller differences. These remaining as they are, they may forward one another in love and in good works.[24]

In this sermon Wesley is dealing with relations among Christians. The fact that we do not all think alike leads to differences in opinions.

Wesley goes on to explain what is implied in "one's heart being right." There are fifty-seven questions asked one after the other. Some relate to beliefs, that is, doctrine. Others relate to the state of one's affections. Others relate to one's behavior. For Wesley, commitment to essential doctrines like the Trinity and divinity of Christ are necessary to one's heart being right. He also condemned latitudinarianism, the idea that it does not matter what one thinks about matters of opinion or which church to attend or how worship should be conducted. Elsewhere in his writings he clearly distinguishes between essential doctrines—those one must believe to be a Christian and those matters of opinion on which Christians can disagree without breaking fellowship. The point of this sermon is that when there is agreement on the essentials, a sincere love should bind Christians together. *Catholic*, as Wesley knew well, means "universal" and he defines catholic spirit in this section:

But while he is steadily fixed in his religious principles, in what he believes to be the truth as it is in Jesus; while he firmly adheres to that worship of God which he judges to be most acceptable in his sight; and while he is united by the tenderest and closest ties to one particular congregation; his heart is enlarged toward all mankind, those he knows and those he does not; he embraces with strong and cordial affection neighbours and strangers, friends and enemies. This is catholic or universal love. And he that has this is of a catholic spirit. For love alone gives the title to this character—catholic love is a catholic spirit.[25]

This catholic love is necessary for Christian unity. But it depends on distinguishing what doctrines and practices are necessary to Christianity or to the existence of a single church, and where Christians can and should respect differing approaches.

This approach to a catholic spirit can be applied to two areas of Christian unity. The unity that exists between Christian churches has a smaller list of requirements. In other words, we can recognize other churches as genuine Christian churches as long as their doctrine does not violate our understanding of essential teachings. They need not share our views on matters of opinion, nor our discipline nor our mission. For example, we count baptism as an essential doctrine and will not recognize as Christian those religions that do not baptize in the name of the triune God. But United Methodists believe that the mode of baptism is a matter of opinion, and we recognize those who profess only believers baptism or only baptism by immersion as fellow Christians. In the area of discipline, a group need not be subject to our General Conference to be counted as *Christians*. We recognize many other Wesleyan bodies let alone other denominational families who have a different ecclesiology from ours. Regarding mission, we think a holistic approach to making disciples of Jesus Christ best summarizes the mission that God has given us. But there are churches that emphasize social justice and others that emphasize evangelism, and we still recognize them as fellow Christians.

But there is also the matter of unity within a single Christian church. There we must have agreement in essential doctrines, a common mission, and a common discipline. Our General Conference defines the limits of variation from these. It defines what are essential doctrines and notes that disseminating teachings contrary to our standards of doctrine is a chargeable offense that warrants being expelled from the ministry or from church membership. Disobedience to the discipline of the church is equally chargeable. Regarding mission, there are many variations on missional emphases, but there are strong covenantal pressures to at least support those aspects of our mission in which one is not directly involved.

Welcome Areas of Diversity

However, the concern for diversity means that there are many areas of the church where diverse expressions of United Methodism are welcome.

WORSHIP

One of the most significant areas of conflict affecting many of our congregations has been labeled "worship wars." Whether the style is high church with much liturgy or contemporary with a praise band or Taizé with much silence or ancient-future in the emergent style, there are many ways in which the Holy Spirit is present in the gathered community and authentic worship occurs. People sense the presence of Christ in worship through many different ways, and our United Methodist denomination has appropriately encouraged diversity. It is expressed in the liturgical structure of the service, in the type of music used, in the way prayer shapes the service and in the physical setting of the worship space. Formality and informality are important variables. For United Methodism to accomplish its mission, it must have many congregations offering worship in many different styles.

Even within one congregation there may be a need for different approaches to worship. One congregation in Wichita, Kansas, has five services each weekend. Saturday night is traditional, three in the sanctuary on Sunday morning are formal traditional, contemporary, and informal traditional; and the youth service in the family life center is aimed at persons fifteen to twenty-nine years old. The sermon in four of the five services is the same every week. It is the other parts of worship that make each one feel different and allow different persons to worship in a style that best relates them to God.

LANGUAGE

Worship is offering praise to God, praying with the gathered community, celebrating the sacraments, and hearing the word of God read and proclaimed. We believe that God can be worshiped in any language, and worship that communicates the praise of the people to God and God's word to the people is authentic. However, there is also value in embodying the catholicity of the Church by letting people sing hymns and hear prayers in languages that belong to their sisters and brothers. For a multicultural congregation, that might be an affirmation and expression of the multilingual makeup of the membership. For any United Methodist church, it can be an expression of our unity in Christ. The United Methodist Church is a global Church worshiping on four continents. Major language groups are English, Spanish, German, French, Swahili, Korean, Russian, Portuguese, Native American tribal languages like Cherokee, and African tribal languages like Shona. For Euro-American people in Kansas to sing a hymn in Swahili or to pray in Spanish (I have seen both done well) is to embody our global unity.

Which language to use is a missional and pastoral judgment that is sometimes difficult. This is especially true in immigrant communities where one generation speaks the language of the old country, the second generation is bilingual, and the third generation knows only the language of the new country. We are committed to embodying the gospel in forms that raise as few barriers as possible in the ministry of evangelism.

But there are other subtleties to language issues. Language about humanity should be gender inclusive, but some communities and age groups care more about this than do others. Further, different audiences have different standards of what constitutes "inclusive." There are various subcultures in the United States that use words in different ways, so that how one speaks the English language can determine the authenticity of one's worship. This is part of the explanation of why so many different English translations of the Bible are in use today.

ETHNICITY

Every church should develop a culture of radical hospitality that genuinely welcomes persons of every ethnic group. Racism and xenophobia (fear of strangers, e.g., immigrants) have no place in the Christian community. No one should be rejected because they are from a different tribe, nation, race, or ethnic group. God welcomes everyone, and so should the Church.

This basic theological commitment can be lived out in at least two different ways. In one, a church like The United Methodist Church can have many different congregations each of which is ethnically homogeneous. Thus, there might be UMC congregations that are black or white or Hispanic or African or Chinese or some other ethnicity. While ethnically homogeneous, each congregation can be sincere in welcoming any persons who want to come. However, given the desires for culturally relevant worship and the role that one's ethnicity plays in cultural commitments, many (and perhaps most) will commit to attending a church that is most comfortable for them. In the United States Christians have developed a denominational pattern of Christianity where individuals seek out which church they wish to attend. Sometimes denominational loyalty is a factor, and persons choose within the denominational family. Increasingly, the denominational label carries less weight.

However, homogenous local churches should find ways to embody ethnic diversity in their ministry. This can be done by inviting persons from different backgrounds to preach, sing, or lead worship on a guest basis. Congregations can hold joint services on special occasions such as Thanksgiving or Ash Wednesday. Participation in an ecumenical organization like the local ministerial alliance can unite all of the different congregations in a city or a region in joint worship or missional service. Leaders attending meetings or annual conference session should intentionally engage fellow United Methodists who represent churches of different backgrounds. Living out our identity as part of the catholic or universal church means intentionally building relationships with people who are different.

But there is another way that our commitment to ethnic diversity can be lived out—the multicultural congregation. Many persons who have attended integrated high schools or served in the armed forces or who work in diverse workplaces also seek out a congregation with various kinds of persons in it. Building a multicultural congregation is a difficult task, but one that can bring significant rewards. Multicultural churches are one of the best expressions of God's plan for humanity.[26] However, Stephen Rhodes also discusses the intentional ways in which leaders of this kind of congregation must address the tensions that exist between the different cultural groups being reached.

OTHER FACTORS

Geography, age, gender, and political persuasion are other factors. We need a church that adapts to different cultural conditions. In my own state, western Kansas is different from Topeka and Kansas City. United Methodists in the Congo are different from those in Southern California. The old who lived through the Depression and World War II are different from my children's generation. Men and women are different, but there are as many expressions of masculinity as there are expressions of femininity. We have liberal Democrats as well as conservative Republicans who belong to the same congregations as well as the same annual conference. President George W. Bush and Senator Hillary Rodham Clinton are both active, faithful United Methodist Christians, and I am proud to be a leader in a church that is big enough to include both.

One of the sinful tendencies of human beings is to seek to limit who God is. We must read the Scriptures and understand the leading of the Holy Spirit over the last two millennia to see that God intends for all sorts of persons to come to have saving faith in Christ and to be made disciples in his church. By valuing diversity of all kinds, we can affirm that God is big enough to welcome everyone.

Limits of Diversity

WORSHIP

Some worship is inauthentic. If it does not name the triune God and if Scripture does not shape it both liturgically and in the reading and preaching of the Word, then what happens is not Christian worship. United Methodists believe in two sacraments, baptism and holy communion, and they should be celebrated in worship as means of grace in which the whole community participates. We do not require that communion be constitutive of every service, but our liturgy presumes that Word and Table is the normal pattern for weekly worship. Wesley's sermon "On Constant Communion" teaches that we ought to receive communion as often as possible. A church that goes through a whole year without ever celebrating communion is not worshiping authentically. Our typical pattern of celebrating once a month is minimal.

Furthermore, there is a desire on the part of many persons to try innovative things in worship. Yet they should be tested against our doctrine. For example, Christian worship should not praise other gods. While we may find value in other religions and seek to build better relationships with Buddhists, Hindus, and Mormons, we should not pray to their gods in our worship services. Scripture is authoritative for our faith, and while other writings can be read and used, it should be clear from our worship that we hold the Bible to be the written word of God. We seek to be inclusive, and our *United Methodist Book of Worship* provides many authentic ways of naming God and minimizing gender and cultural bias in worship. However, the triune God must be clearly the one worshiped.

When one congregation has many different worship styles, the question must be asked: How do these different services work together for the unity of the congregation? Having the same sermon at all services is helpful here. Having similar clergy leadership is helpful. There are other ways of ensuring the unity of the congregation despite different worship experiences, but preserving that unity when there are different gatherings of the congregation is an important concern.

LANGUAGE

Worship should be in the language the people understand. One of the principle changes made by Protestants in the Reformation was to conduct worship in the language of the people. They thought that Latin-language liturgies were not the way Christians should worship. In addition, they believed that the Bible should be accessible to the people in the vernacular, and Protestants took great risks to translate and publish the Scriptures for the people. Our modern commitment to this same principle includes the use of visual media for worship, so that generations raised watching television and now using the Internet can hear and see the gospel through multisensory worship.

At the same time, there is a risk in encouraging such diversity in languages. Too often, we have lost a common vocabulary for the faith. There was a time when key words such as *salvation, sin, justification, sanctification, trinity,* and *evangelism* were used with roughly similar meanings so that people could understand each other. Such a common range of meanings enabled genuine disagreements to be voiced and conversations held. When we use different languages, even different dialects of English, we should seek to maintain a common vocabulary for the sake of our community.

ETHNICITY

Far too often our commitment to the catholicity of the church is weak. We have grown up or come to faith within a particular expression of Christianity, and we know deep in our hearts that God was present there and this was the right way to worship and to serve the Lord. Thus, we presume that authentic Christianity is just like our congregation. The ethnocentric approach thinks and perhaps says out loud, "All of those other people are welcome to become Christians if they worship and serve just like we do." The most common and unfortunate expression of this trend is in our cities where a church of one ethnicity finds that its neighborhood has changed and the persons who might join as new members don't share the same cultural values as the existing congregation. The congregation must either change or die, and the group's commitment to being a homogeneous unit leads to the congregation's death. If on the other hand, it is willing to change, it must see that either a new homogeneous approach or a multicultural approach needs to be taken.

The other limit to diversity for ethnicity is that sometimes Christians are prepared to sacrifice essential teachings or practices in the name of cultural inclusiveness. When I was young, a daring youth minister served what he called holy communion by using potato chips and Coca-Cola. I did not then and do not now believe that was Holy Communion—Scripture is clear about the elements of bread and wine. Some believe that we United Methodists have violated Scripture by using unfermented wine, an option not available to Jesus at the Last Supper. On that point our church has said adaptation to a society pervaded by alcohol abuse requires a special kind of wine—the unfermented juice of the grape.

OTHER FACTORS

One of the sinful tendencies of human beings is to make universal claims for our particular form of Christianity. We have already discussed several factors that might cause us to limit God's work. Geography, age, gender, and political persuasion are other factors. There is another tendency, however, which is to overvalue diversity. We might say that anything goes and each subgroup, however defined, is sufficient unto itself.

In reality, our diversity makes sense only within the limits of Christian unity. Each person might prefer her or his own expression of United Methodism, but it is important to know that one's expression is only one among many legitimate ones, and to know where the boundary is beyond which one cannot go and still be an authentic United Methodist congregation.

Two Legitimate Grounds for Schism

Our unity as The United Methodist Church is constituted by our doctrine, our mission, and our discipline. Schism, or splitting the church, is an intentional decision to violate the discipline of the Church. Whether the separation is amicable or not, the schism results in different polities, different decision-making structures, and different actions. For example, the separation of the Church of England from the Roman Catholic Church was a decision taken by the English Catholics not to accept the Roman Church's authority. There were many issues involved; and historians debate whether doctrine, worship, or Henry VIII's divorce was the key factor. The larger context of developing nation-states, European disunity, the moral decline of the Renaissance papacy, and the invention of cheap printing technology further enabled this conflict to take the course that it did.

It is possible for a schism to be mostly about discipline. The desire for power and dominance by one person over others or by one group over others is a factor in the history of many groups. Some would even suggest that the desire for dominance is the most significant reason and so most of the conversation should be about power relationships. Any realistic analysis of our current situation as United Methodists must take that into account as well.

But I am seeking to address thoughtful people who would not intentionally seek power for its own sake. Rather, we are seeking to do what is best for God's Church and to obey the commands of Christ. While being attentive to issues of discipline and power, we seek to ask for the highest and best reasons for using what power and decision-making processes we have. Our discipline should serve the doctrine and mission of the Church.

Toward that end, the question arises: Is it ever permissible to split the church? Clearly it has been done, but do we today judge that these schisms were good or bad actions? Ecumenically minded Christians are torn today by acknowledging that some good has come out of these divisions while working diligently to heal the brokenness they have caused. What would the Catholic Church have been like, for example, had the Protestants not left in the sixteenth century? With Lutherans and Calvinists present at the Council of Trent, the whole course of Europe and modern Christianity would have been altered significantly.

A balanced, historical view of separation was offered by Archbishop Rowan Williams at the signing of a covenant between the Church of England and the Methodist Church of Great Britain. He is quoted in an ecumenical dialogue report:

> Neither Methodists nor Catholics should regard their separation as acceptable. Some may believe that certain separations were necessary in the past for the sake of the Gospel. Others may view all separations as failures by one party or the other, or indeed both, which have obscured the unity of Christ's Church. In 2003, the Archbishop of Canterbury said of the divided histories of the Church of England and the Methodist Church of Great Britain: "Wesley came to the point where he believed that he and his followers could only be fully obedient to Jesus Christ if they took the risk of separation. No-one can

easily pass judgement on this costly decision, and no-one is seeking to do so; what we can be sure of is that by God's direction it bore fruit in witness and transforming service to the Kingdom of God in this nation and far beyond."[27]

Archbishop Williams called the split of Methodism away from the Church of England "costly." In many ways, both sides were impoverished. At the same time, thoughtful ecumenists can now value what God has done through separated churches, and the point of the Commission's report is to see these different developments as gifts to be received through greater unity.

Can such gifts be retained and recognized without going through a costly schism? That is the point of my contribution to this book—I believe they can. But here we must acknowledge that separation is sometimes necessary, and we should be clear about the criteria for making that decision.

John Wesley defined schism as "a causeless separation from a body of living Christians." He went on to say,

> And it is certain all the members of Christian communities should be carefully guarded against it. For how little a thing soever it may seem, and how innocent soever it may be accounted, schism, even in this sense, is both evil in itself, and productive of evil consequences.[28]

Wesley goes on to argue that a causeless separation is a breach of the law of love.

> It is only when our love grows cold that we can think of separating from our brethren. And this is certainly the case with any who willingly separate from their Christian brethren. The pretences for separation may be innumerable, but want of love is always the real cause; otherwise they would still hold the unity of the spirit in the bond of peace.[29]

But a little later in the sermon Wesley acknowledges two different grounds that would justify separation.

> Suppose, for instance, you were a member of the Church of Rome, and you could not remain therein without committing idolatry, without worshipping of idols, whether images or saints and angels; then it would be your bounden duty to leave that community, totally to separate from

45

it. Suppose you could not remain in the Church of England without doing something which the Word of God forbids, or omitting something which the Word of God positively commands; if this were the case (but blessed be God it is not) you ought to separate from the Church of England.[30]

This is basically doctrinal—if one's church forces one to violate essential doctrines like the Ten Commandments or to violate the clear teaching of Scripture, one is justified in separating from it.

He continues,

> To be more particular. I know God has committed to me a dispensation of the gospel. Yea, and my own salvation depends upon preaching it: 'Woe is me, if I preach not the gospel.' If then I could not remain in the Church without omitting this, without desisting from preaching the gospel, I should be under a necessity of separating from it, or losing my own soul. In like manner, if I could not continue united to any smaller society, church, or body of Christians, without committing sin, without lying and hypocrisy, without preaching to others doctrines which I did not myself believe, I should be under an absolute necessity of separating from that society. And in all these cases the sin of separation, with all the evils consequent upon it, would not lie upon me, but upon those who constrained me to make that separation by requiring of me such terms of communion as I could not in conscience comply with.[31]

This argument is essentially missional. If the Church had forbidden Wesley to preach out of doors and to form societies, he would have left because he had a clear mission to reach those outside the current worshiping congregations of the Church of England. In fact, while one bishop told him to quit preaching in his diocese and another attacked him in a publication, no one took any ecclesiastical action to prevent Wesley from carrying out his mission. On his understanding, he lived and died a faithful minister of the Church of England. Methodism was a movement within the Church in that country. The separation of the American Methodists in 1784 was due, in his view, completely to the separation of the American colonies from the mother country, and Wesley could not envision their relationship to the Church of England continuing.

Another important source for discussing the unity of the UMC today was given in 1998 by a dialogue group organized by the General Commission on Christian Unity and Interreligious Concerns. Its report, called "In Search of Unity," analyzed the issues and offered recommendations. It notes that "The unity of the church is a gift of the Triune God through the working of the Holy Spirit. As such this gift is a great treasure which is intrinsically worthwhile. It also brings great benefits, not least its role to make Christ more manifest in the world (John 17)."[32] The report discusses two "Challenges that Harbor the Danger of Explicit Disunity or Schism," namely "Different Understandings of the Authority of Scripture and Divine Revelation" and "Disagreement over the Boundaries of the Church."[33] In theological terms, they are suggesting that the tensions the church faces over homosexuality are actually deeper than only that issue and involve the doctrines of Scripture and the Church.

In line with Wesley's teaching and the dialogue group's analysis, then, I suggest that there are two legitimate reasons why one might split from the Church: if the Church teaches doctrines that are contrary to the essential doctrines of the faith, and if the Church prevents you from being in mission to persons whom God requires you to reach.

TEACHING CONTRARY TO ESSENTIAL DOCTRINES

To make the point of doctrinal integrity clear, let me use the doctrine of the Trinity. What would be a faithful response if The United Methodist Church were to amend the Articles of Religion and Confession of Faith (Articles I-IV and Confession I-III) to say "We are in disagreement about the nature of God and whether the idea of one God in three persons and the divinity of Jesus Christ are the correct way to interpret Scripture, and so we agree to disagree on this teaching"? Essentially this would give official sanction to Unitarian theology. Our desire for inclusiveness would mean that official Sunday school literature, hymnals, the next Book of Worship, and official pronouncements would need to be worded in such a way that persons of a Unitarian persuasion would not be offended. Seminaries accredited by the University Senate would need to have

Unitarian theologians on their faculties. General Conference would have the opportunity for deep theological debate about how best to word our understanding of God's essence so that we can say as much as possible together without violating our desire to "agree to disagree."

Such a situation would be intolerable. It would violate the church's understanding of Scripture and would wreck the progress made in ecumenical dialogue over the last century. To worship a God who is not triune is to worship a different God. We make a clear exception for Jews, because Scripture itself teaches us that Judaism worships the same God we do and we are wild olive branches grafted onto their tree (Romans 9–11). But Unitarians and followers of other religions that do not acknowledge that Jesus Christ is God incarnate cannot be included as members of the Christ's Church.

The General Conference of 2000 adopted a resolution saying that members of the Church of Jesus Christ of Latter-day Saints should be given Christian baptism when they seek to become members of The United Methodist Church. This directive has many reasons behind it, but the doctrine of the trinity is a key one. Mormons believe in three gods and that the divine persons they call Father, Son, and Holy Spirit are three separate entities. In addition, any male can become a god by making sufficient spiritual progress. Thus, when Mormons are given what their religion calls "baptism," we believe and teach that this ceremony is not Christian baptism because it is not done in the name of the Triune God. Hence, coming to The United Methodist Church they are not being rebaptized, but being baptized for the first time.

It is thus imperative that we distinguish which doctrines are essential and which are not. The United Methodist Church is not as clear about this matter as it should be, and there is some confusion about it. However, we do use the term "standards of doctrine," which points to the source of our essential teachings. I have also argued that our doctrinal standards stand in need of revision to change their language and express the same essential doctrines more clearly for the twenty-first century. I believe they would function better in all the ways that doctrinal standards are supposed to function for our denomination if they were in a different form.

However, if a revision process were to substantially alter something like the doctrine of the Trinity, that would be sufficient cause for schism.

There are specific teachings within our doctrinal standards, however, that in my view do not rise to the level of essential doctrines. Wesley's views on the Second Coming of Christ, contained in his notes on Revelation, cause difficulties today.[34] In addition, the anti–Roman Catholic Articles in the Articles of Religion could be restated in light of our best ecumenical insights. With regard to things that separated the Church of England from the Roman Catholics in the sixteenth century (when this language was first formulated), our two churches have come to clearer and deeper understandings of each other's positions. The recent Joint Declaration on the Doctrine of Justification, signed on our behalf by the World Methodist Council and thereby joining the Lutheran World Federation and the Roman Catholic Church, shows how ecumenical progress can be made.

MISSIONAL IMPERATIVES

Methodism as a church was born out of missional imperative not out of doctrinal dispute. In separating from the Church of England, we had no irresolvable disputes with the official teachings of the Church of England. We did have differences in emphasis, notably on the witness of the Spirit and Christian perfection, but both of the Wesley brothers believed they could wholeheartedly support the Articles, Homilies, and Liturgy of their church.

Methodism gradually grew away from its mother church because of its mission of reaching those outside the church. Methodists might blame the Church of England's failure to adapt to new cultural realities (internal migration within England and the separation of the American colonies), and Anglicans might blame Methodist impatience and lack of concern for unity. Nevertheless, the split should be understood as arising primarily out of different understandings about the mission of the church. The early Methodists received a great deal of criticism for field preaching and society meetings. Many of their new converts did not feel welcome in the parish churches and over time began to hold preaching services at the same time as worship in the parish church. John and Charles Wesley continually fought against the drift toward separation, but over time it became overwhelming.

One might argue that similar developments over the last forty years in the United States have occurred. Because the UMC has not moved quickly enough in mission to certain groups outside our church, some United Methodists have left the denomination because of God's call on their lives to be in ministry with these people. One can argue that we have not done an adequate job of reaching youth, college students, gays and lesbians, the military, evangelicals, environmentalists, and others. Thus, we find former United Methodists who are actively serving God as clergy and laity in other Christian churches and parachurch organizations.

In my view, we have not formally refused to be in ministry with anyone. Once again, let me take an obvious case as an illustration. Consider the extreme case that we as a Church would decide that no college student would be allowed to worship in our services while they were in school, and that their membership would be suspended from the time they left their parents' home until the time they were employed and self-sufficient. If that were to happen, many of us might leave the Church in order to be campus ministers and make disciples among college students. In such a case, schism would be justified because of a missional imperative and the Church's official and clear refusal to be the means of grace to these people.

However, such a step has not been taken. Instead, one might argue that a more subtle series of decisions has characterized our ministry with this group. We have in many cases failed to adapt our worship to their culture. We have been slow to put screens and projectors in our sanctuaries. In too many cases we have not given adequate support to our Wesley Foundations and have not sent our best and most talented clergy to be in ministry there. We have not formed sufficiently large young adult groups in our congregations. Without officially rejecting this group, we have practically neglected them in too many places. (Please note that there are many places in the United States where United Methodists are doing excellent ministry with college students, but the overall trend is far below what we need.) Thus, the average age of United Methodists is far above the average age of our general population.

Would schism be acceptable here? I believe not. I believe that a concern for the unity of the Church and for the salvation of college students would lead a thoughtful person to remain in The United Methodist Church and work to change its ministry in this area. To split off and form a parachurch campus ministry organization is to cut the ties of college students to the established Church and to deprive them of many of the means of grace that God intends Christians to receive. The answer in this case is to renew and revitalize the Church's ministry in this important area.

Six Key Issues

I want to discuss six divisive issues facing The United Methodist Church today and the idea that our diversity might be compatible with our commitment to unity. In each of these cases there are persons in our denomination who are passionately committed to different and conflicting positions. In each of these I will argue that the truth lies in the extreme center and that our commitment to unity is an important and often overlooked part of the mix. When one party focuses on just one issue and particularly on their views on that issue as the only one, then the good of the whole is often lost. Standing in the extreme center means holding a variety of different positions in tension with each other. We as United Methodists are committed to preaching and the sacraments, to evangelism and social justice, to leadership of both lay and clergy, to justification and sanctification, to social justice positions some of which are conservative and some of which are liberal.

My analyses of each of these issues have similar logical patterns that can be summarized in four points:

1. The issue is complex and is usually distorted by slogans or deeply
   held views most clearly articulated by one side or the other.

2. There is a balanced, centrist position that if carefully articulated provides a powerful Christian response.
3. The Church should teach and live by the extreme centrist position, but know that our life as a Church is enriched and enhanced by the views expressed by more extreme positions on both sides.
4. Mission unifies.

The General Conference Unity Resolution lifted up the mission of the Church as more important than any one of the dividing issues.

RACE AND GENDER

Racism is a sin that plagues American culture and infects the life of the Church. The practice of slavery characterized the founding of the American colonies and shaped the cultures of many of our states. Euro-American immigrants mistreated the Indians already living in America. While the oppression of black persons and native persons has a huge place in our history, racism today also affects persons of every color and taints relationships between many different groups.

Racism has affected the unity of Methodism. Early in the nineteenth century the African Methodist Episcopal Church and the African Methodist Episcopal Zion Church split off from the Methodist Episcopal Church. The MEC divided in 1844 between North and South, with slavery as the main cause. The Christian Methodist Episcopal Church separated from the southern church at the end of the Civil War. Our efforts at unity bore fruit with union in 1939, but African Americans were segregated into a Central Jurisdiction. It is significant that no African American delegate to the 1939 General Conference voted for the union because of this segregation. It was within my lifetime that we finally ended official segregation.

Racism has been defined in our Social Principles as "the combination of the power to dominate by one race over other races and a value system that assumes that the dominant race is innately superior to the others" (*Book of Discipline*, ¶162A). It is wrong in both its personal and institutional manifestations. It should not characterize the thoughts or behavior of individuals or our decisions as a Church. Sometimes there are decisions made or actions taken that are clearly racist and should be resisted.

In a similar way, sexism is a sin. Women have been oppressed for centuries and only in recent times has the Church and society made steps to recognize their equality with men. Opportunities once denied women, such as ordination and leadership of institutions, have only recently been made available to them. The struggle for gender equity continues.

But what characterizes the life of our Church and American culture generally is much more subtle than that, and in many cases it is not clear which decision best avoids racism or sexism. The hardest decisions come with regard to personnel. One extreme position says that we should promote, elect, or choose persons who will advance the presence of oppressed groups in leadership. We value diversity so highly that it is important that we have women and persons of color in those places regardless of qualifications and we are satisfied if the gender/ethnic makeup is right. The opposite extreme position says that we have resolved issues of racial prejudice and gender bias, and that we should judge only on the basis of qualifications. This position argues that tokenism and filling quotas are racist and sexist.

The centrist position here is that one's gender or race is one of the qualifications that should be considered. Sending a white clergywoman to serve as senior pastor of a large African American church may make a statement about inclusiveness and open itineracy, and it may be the right appointment to make. However, her gender and her race are not incidental and unimportant factors in her ability to serve successfully in that church. In the case of any one individual being considered for any particular appointment, the mix of qualifications is important to consider. Another aspect of the centrist position is that multicultural denominations are closer to God's plan for humanity than are predominantly monocultural denominations. While there are many historic barriers of racism and cultural oppression still to be overcome, the goal of Christian unity envisions a church that embraces persons of all different races and ethnicities.

SCRIPTURE

The Articles of Religion and Confession of Faith are quite clear that Scripture is our authority in matters of faith and practice. Article V says,

> The Holy Scripture containeth all things necessary to salvation; so that whatsoever is not read therein, nor may be proved thereby, is not to be required of any man that it should be believed as an article of faith, or be thought requisite or necessary to salvation. (*Book of Discipline*, 60)

In similar words Confession IV says that it "reveals the Word of God so far as it is necessary for our salvation. It is to be received through the Holy Spirit as the true rule and guide for faith and practice" (*Book of Discipline*, 67). Our official doctrine already occupies the extreme center in the careful distinctions it makes. Note that there is no claim to inerrancy, nor is there any claim to be authoritative in scientific matters. Rather, it contains what we human beings need to know for salvation and guides our faith and practice.

A more extreme position teaches inerrancy and argues that belief in Scripture's authority requires that one reject modern scientific understandings of evolution. It would argue for a dictation theory of revelation and draw a tight identification between the words of the Bible and God's Word.

The other extreme position would argue that the Bible is just another humanly produced historical document that the church happened to canonize and that it should be taken as one source of our teachings alongside other equally important sources. From 1972 to 1988 Part II of the *Discipline*, in a section called "Our Theological Task" offered a variety of formulations of how Scripture, tradition, reason, and experience were to be used. A number of leaders in our Church, seeking to counteract the abuses of Scripture that were currently being taught in various places, offered the perspective that Scripture could be outvoted by the other three. The *Discipline's* own language contributed to that by saying,

> These four norms for doctrinal formulations are not simply parallel and none can be subsumed by any other. There is a primacy that goes with Scripture, as the constitutive witness to biblical wellsprings of our faith.

> In practice, however, theological reflection may find its point of departure in tradition, "experience," or rational analysis. What matters most is that all four guidelines be brought to bear upon every doctrinal consideration. (*Book of Discipline*, 1972 ¶70)

Note that the *Discipline* did not say, "What matters most is faithfulness to Scripture properly interpreted." Instead, for sixteen years the church emphasized the four sources as co-equal norms of faith. They have been known popularly as the "Wesleyan Quadrilateral" even though the phrase has never been used in any *Book of Discipline* and Wesley scholars have argued that the Church's teaching misrepresented Wesley's views.[35] Confusion about scriptural authority has led to confusion about how best to think about difficult issues. During that period of time, one United Methodist leader once wrote, "I ran the issue of homosexuality through the quadrilateral, and Scripture lost, three to one."[36] This view of Scripture's relation to reason, tradition, and experience clearly violates the doctrinal standards of the Church.

The extreme center position is to affirm that the Bible alone is our authority, but it is never alone. It should be interpreted with reason, tradition, and experience, properly employed. The difficulties arise in specifying how they should interrelate. Modern science has posed many of the most difficult challenges to scriptural authority, breaking down the worldview based on biblical chronologies that the earth was created in 4004 B.C. But cultural changes of all sorts, including feminism, restrictions on war, capitalism, and democracy have caused Christians to adapt biblical teachings to new cultural realities. When we do so, we must do it in harmony with the basic teachings and overall thrust of the Bible. John Wesley called this "the general tenor" of Scripture.[37] Thus, the argument for the ordination of women is based primarily, in my view, on the general tenor of the New Testament not to allow gender differences to block God's saving activity through the church. There are specific texts that support women prophesying and others that proclaim the equality of women and men in Christ. But the general tenor of Christ's ministry and the sweep of the New Testament was to make salvation available to all and to create community where persons were in leadership by virtue of their gifts without regard to their gender or nationality. This is not an argument that "the Bible is out of date." It is an argument that faithfulness to Scripture should always have led Christians to ordain women, and now a changed cultural situation allows us to take that important step.

CHRISTOLOGY

The two most fundamental questions that shape Christian witness today are "Does God exist?" and "Who is Jesus?" The first question addresses rising secularism and atheism that suggests that there is no God at all. The second question addresses what kind of God there is and specifically whether Jesus of Nazareth was God incarnate who continues to be alive today. The Nicene Creed is our touchstone for this. We Christians say we believe in one God in three persons as a way of summarizing the teaching of Scripture.

Two mistakes are frequently made with regard to how the Church talks about Jesus. On the one side, we sometimes treat Jesus as a merely human teacher. On the other side, we sometimes talk about Jesus as a separate divine entity, with our language and our prayers appearing to believe in three gods. We correct this every time we pray the Great Thanksgiving of the communion ritual in a trinitarian way.[38] Charles Wesley's hymns such as "Maker, in Whom We Live" give a full account of how the three persons are all one. The second and fourth stanzas make the point:

> Incarnate Deity, let all the ransomed race render in thanks their lives to thee for thy redeeming grace. The grace to sinners showed ye heavenly choirs proclaim, and cry, "Salvation to our God, salvation to the Lamb!"

> Eternal, Triune God, let all the hosts above, let all on earth below record and dwell upon thy love. When heaven and earth are fled before thy glorious face, sing all the saints thy love hath made thine everlasting praise.[39]

There are many orthodox Christologies. Some of them emphasize Jesus' humanity without losing sight of his divinity. Others emphasize his divinity while acknowledging and giving appropriate recognition to his humanity. More recently, different theologies have sought to give emphasis to the various human perspectives from which Jesus is viewed, noting differences of class, gender, race, nationality, and other distinguishing factors. A great argument for why diversity within the Church is important can be made by noting how all of these different perspectives enhance our understanding of the scriptural account of Christ. All too often we tend to re-invent Christ in our own image rather than seeking to read the scriptural text in the many different ways found in the entire Church.

At the same time, there must be basic agreement on the most important aspects of Christology for the unity of the Church. The Nicene Creed sets boundaries for the conversation about how best to understand Christ. The second person of the Trinity is truly God, of one being with the Father. Christ existed before creation and became incarnate for humanity's salvation. He truly died, was buried, and rose again on the third day. Within those boundaries, Christianity has encouraged and welcomed many different theologies; and great progress has been made by different theologians testing the boundaries and occasionally crossing them. However, the unity of the church requires that essential christological teachings be upheld so that we are all saying "Jesus is Lord" together.

HOMOSEXUALITY

Perhaps nothing has been more divisive for United Methodists in my lifetime than the issue of homosexuality. It first got serious attention at the 1972 General Conference when a study committee on Social Principles addressed the issue. The General Conferences since then (eight more of them) have addressed the issue in a variety of ways. The Church's basic position has been clarified without substantially changing. Despite the consistency of the Church's teaching, many persons on both sides continue to strongly object to it.

The Church's clearest teaching on this issue is contained in its Social Principles, ¶161G. It says,

> Homosexual persons no less than heterosexual persons are individuals
> of sacred worth. All persons need the ministry and guidance of the

church in their struggles for human fulfillment, as well as the spiritual and emotional care of a fellowship that enables reconciling relationships with God, with others, and with self. The United Methodist Church does not condone the practice of homosexuality and consider this practice incompatible with Christian teaching. We affirm that God's grace is available to all, and we will seek to live together in Christian community. We implore families and churches not to reject or condemn lesbian and gay members and friends. We commit ourselves to be in ministry for and with all persons. (*Book of Discipline*, ¶161)

There are many persons who are deeply opposed to the balanced view of this statement. On one side, there are persons who believe that God calls all persons to resist whatever immoral drives and impulses may exist in our sinful human nature. They believe that Scripture, supported and interpreted properly by reason, tradition, and experience, teaches that homosexual behavior is always immoral. While persons holding this view support the Church's teaching that homosexual practice is incompatible with Christian teaching, they believe our best ministry with persons is to issue a clearer call to fidelity in heterosexual marriage or celibacy in singleness. They deplore the double standard whereby some congregations accept self-avowed, practicing lesbian, gay, bisexual, and transgender (LGBT) persons as members while rejecting such persons from ordained ministry. They believe the balanced position of our Social Principles mutes the call for high moral standards to be lived out by all Christians. Many of them would say that while homosexuality is not the most important moral issue facing American culture today (some would point to racism, poverty, materialism, divorce, abortion, and other issues) they believe they must respond to organized campaigns from those groups that are seeking to weaken the Church's historic teaching.

On the other side, persons supporting full rights for LGBT persons believe that these orientations and gender identities are gifts from God and that the Church should teach that there are ways to live in these relationships with faithfulness and moral integrity. Some believe that LGBT persons constitute an oppressed class and that the gospel's word to them promises liberation. Thus, to exclude them from ordination and to refuse to perform marriage or union ceremonies for them is a violation of

God's all-embracing love. To distinguish between orientation and practice is to put an unbearable burden of celibacy upon persons that is not being asked of heterosexually oriented persons. Thus, the Church's position on homosexuality is just one more imperfection in its witness and life. The struggle for full LGBT rights is part of a broader witness for justice in the world. In this view, when the Church eventually decides to ordain practicing homosexuals and perform same-gender marriage services, we will be embodying the love and grace of Christ more fully than we do now. Persons in this group are often committed to a long-term struggle to correct this historic wrong being done to LGBT persons, but they expect God to lead the Church to full justice for them.

Another group of persons believes that the UMC's current statement is coherent and faithful and should be maintained. From this perspective the statement has several advantages. First, it is faithful to biblical teaching. They say that a careful reading of Scripture does not support same-gender sexual relationships and that many key texts condemn it. This view believes it is God's intention that sexual relationships should be confined to marriage between one man and one woman. Persons in this group often hold the view that homosexual practice is a choice for some, and they believe that changing the Church's teaching would bless immoral behaviors and thereby invite many others into them. These are questions that go deep into discussions about sexual orientations, freedom of the will, and the possibility of God's assisting persons to change. Second, the nature of leadership of our Church, and particularly the ministry of those called to preach the gospel, requires that leaders convey this message in word and action. The Church should intentionally hold clergy to a higher standard of behavior because they embody the witness of the Church in the way that lay members do not. The Church should be prepared to be in ministry with LGBT persons and to accept them as members because it believes that God's grace is at work in everyone's life and everyone needs the means of grace that only the Church provides. Third, this group believes our current statement preserves our doctrinal understanding that all Christians are in a process of salvation, and that the power of sin is diminishing in human lives so that disciples are moving on toward Christian maturity. Persons affirming the faithfulness and coherence of our current teaching might say that many human beings struggle with deep-rooted sins that affect our ability to lead the Church. For many of these sins, there is a line between acknowledging one's own sinfulness and proclaiming that the given behavior is not really a sin. Consider the case of unrepentant greed. Some leaders in our Church are greedy. But if someone were to cross the line and begin teaching that greed is not a sin or that persons who generously give away all that they can are inferior to others, their leadership in the Church would not be tolerated. On this view, our statement allows for the Church to be in ministry with lesbian, gay, bisexual, and transgender persons without proclaiming that their behaviors are compatible with Christian teaching.

This summary of three different approaches to the issue of homosexuality is overly simplistic, and there are many different shades and combinations of views not fully represented in them. But I believe the unity of the Church is best served if persons holding all three of these perspectives are included in our Church. We need those who seek to change the Church's teaching to be more strict about sexual morality. They are advocates for moral clarity and consistency in a world where compromises about sexual morality are too easily made. We need those who seek to change the Church's teaching to be more accepting of LGBT behaviors. They are in touch with groups of persons who need the ministry of the Church and who are often misunderstood by others. We also need to affirm the broad middle of the Church that seeks to love everyone and to minister to everyone while affirming traditional Christian teaching. If any one of these groups were to decide to leave because the struggle was too hard, the rest of the Church would be impoverished.

Is this a Church-dividing issue? I believe it is. I believe that the lessons of the Episcopal Church in the United States are clear that if a church's practice changes in the way that theirs has changed, schism results. We can continue with our current teaching without schism. People who cannot remain because the Church is too liberal or too conservative will leave. But thousands of gay and lesbian members are willing to remain in The United Methodist Church with its current teaching, and after thirty-four years many of them know that the likelihood of change is quite small. Some stay because they believe it is a generational issue and the next group will change the Church's position. Others have reconciled to the idea that the Church will not change its position and have decided to stay regardless. Thousands of conservatives are willing to stay as long as the teaching is right and there is no chance of self-avowed practicing homosexuals serving as clergy. They also know that the debate will continue for many more years and they are prepared to belong to a Church that is willing to discuss matters like this.

Should homosexuality be a Church-dividing issue? The document "In Search of Unity" draws an interesting distinction to help answer this question. In the section headed "Disagreement Over the Boundaries of the Church" it says,

> There are those who in conscience can accept the continuation of divergent points of view within the church structure and those who in conscience cannot. Within each of these groups—compatibilists and incompatibilists—we can identify people representing perspectives which are both "more liberal" and "more conservative."[40]

The distinction is helpful because there are those who cannot tolerate one church that has members who disagree over this issue. There are those who welcome the wide range of views held by United Methodists. There are yet others who will tolerate diverse views so long as the Church's official teaching agrees with their view and they will not get a pastor of their Church whose practice contradicts the Church's moral standards.

On the issue of homosexuality, I am a compatibilist. I welcome diverse opinions and conversation because I think the Church needs the conversation. This is only possible because I do not regard our teaching on homosexuality as an essential doctrine. However, when arguments are put forward for changing our teaching with perspectives that do violate our essential doctrines, then the nature of the discussion has shifted. Those who seek to change our Church's teaching must do so on the basis of scriptural authority as interpreted by our doctrinal standards.

GLOBAL NATURE

One of the most important challenges facing Christianity today is globalization. The world is becoming more and more interrelated, with both good and bad aspects of that process. We are more deeply connected by technology, communication, travel, and common issues such as global warming and terrorism. If Christ's church is one, how do we best embody that unity?

There are some who hope earnestly for the unity of all Christians, and so they have put great emphasis on broad-based ecumenical organizations such as the World Council of Churches. Others have thought that denominational families such as the World Methodist Council are the best approach. This perspective says that national identities are important, and that Christian unity ought to follow national lines and then find some visible ecumenical expression in a loose association of nationally based churches. Many Christian bodies, such as Southern Baptists, Anglicans, Lutherans, and the Reformed have formed loose associations that have multinational impact without being one church.

The Roman Catholic Church and The United Methodist Church are two global denominations. In each case they share the same doctrine, mission, and discipline to a degree that means they are one church operating on many different continents. The United Methodist Council of Bishops includes persons who superintend our ministry on four continents. The United Methodist General Conference discerns God's will and determines our discipline and doctrine for the United Methodists in more than fifty countries speaking many different languages.

The missionary movement of previous centuries has borne great fruit, and we now find the Church in Africa and Asia rapidly outgrowing the Church in North America and Europe. Our structures as a United Methodist Church have failed to keep pace with our new reality. We too often behave as if the UMC is an American denomination with a few foreign mission stations. The number of General Conference delegates from Central Conferences will approach 20 percent in 2008 and is expected to be higher in 2012. Delegates from outside the United

States complain that too much time is spent on U.S. issues, and U.S. delegates complain that there is no forum where U.S. issues can be dealt with by U.S. representatives.

Many different ideas have been proposed over the last several decades for how we should adjust. Too often they have been attached to complex proposals and have been defeated because of the other ideas that are not ready to be adopted. I believe great progress can be made if the General Conference will create a Central Conference for the United States, and then determine the answers to two questions:

1. What paragraphs of our *Book of Discipline* are applicable to all United Methodists everywhere, i.e., they are global.
2. What paragraphs of our *Book of Discipline* ought to be regionally determined, that is, settled by Central Conferences.

In such a proposal many things would remain the same: the number and powers of jurisdictions in the United States, the number and responsibilities of general agencies, the determination of the Church's doctrine and Social Principles being determined by the General Conference; the size and makeup of the General Conference all would be untouched by such a proposal. How General Conference will look at this is yet to be determined. Even if something like this is passed, the question of how best to embody our unity as a global Church will be a continuing question for the rest of this century.

THE GIFT OF UNITY AND HOLY COMMUNION

Unity is not the same as uniformity. We have seen how important diversity is to the body of Christ. Diversity includes spiritual gifts, ethnicities, cultures, languages, and theological persuasions within the boundaries of our doctrine, discipline, and mission. Yet one of the most powerfully unifying moments in the life of the Church—local church, annual conference, central conference, or General Conference—is the sacrament of holy communion where the celebrant says,

Because there is one loaf,
we, who are many, are one body, for we all partake of the one loaf.
The bread which we break is a sharing in the body of Christ.[41]

People of different races, different nationalities, different theological persuasions, and people of different generations all hear the gospel word proclaimed and then partake sacramentally of Christ's body and blood. God's grace is a unifying force we cannot begin to understand, but we come to the table repeatedly because it is our very life being given to us.

As a Wesleyan, I can believe only that our failure to embody this unity means we are not yet mature. Mature Christians understand how the unity of the Church is necessary to our mission and our very identity as the body of Christ. If this unity is the deepest truth of our existence as Christ's disciples, as members of his body, then we must wrestle with the question: **How do we live more fully into this gift of unity?**

CHAPTER TWO

RESPONSES TO "GOD'S GIFT OF UNITY"

WILLIAM J. ABRAHAM

Bishop Scott Jones is a nimble theologian and a Cadillac ecclesiastical politician. I applaud his effort to tackle an elusive problem in United Methodism. He has delivered a homiletical ramble; this genre has its limitations, but it explores the issues in an accessible way. Those familiar with Bishop Jones's writings will find few surprises. Yet he has woven his convictions into a new tapestry.

I welcome his concern about the division of United Methodism. It is a miracle that we remain united; division is a looming specter in the churches of the West; United Methodists who think we are exceptional live in a fantasy world. The hasty unity resolution of the 2004 Conference was a glaring manifestation of an acute problem; it was not a solution. Bishop Jones's solution has various dimensions. Heed the command of Scripture to visible unity, value diversity and inclusiveness, attend to Wesley's conception of commands as implicit promises, realize that the unity of the Church is an apt response to the polarizations of the world, and so on.

The pace picks up when we catch Bishop Jones's vision of mission. Unity, he says, is crucial to the mission of the Church. Empirically this is false; divisions have at times been extremely effective evangelistically. I am willing to bet a month's salary that the Anglican Church that emerges out of the Episcopal shenanigans will grow exponentially over the next century in the United States. The issue is not division *per se* but devotion to the faith and to the practices of evangelism; if commitment to the latter causes division, then we may see the Church flourish in mission. Bishop Jones wobbles at this point. The Church "shares in the two natures that characterized Jesus Christ . . . the Church is fully human and fully divine." This is not the faith of the Church. Furthermore, his startling claim has immediate problems for his general thesis. If it is true, the unity of the Church is an accomplished reality; we do not need to work at it at all, whether motivated by mission or not. Moreover, the qualifications he makes will undermine the high Christology, if we do not keep our wits about us. There is worse to come: "Where Christ is present, the Church is energized to participate in God's mission of saving the world." This time it is the work of Christ that is compromised, as if the Church can add to the once-for-all saving work of Christ in his cross and resurrection! Happily Bishop Jones is on the side of the angels in the end. He really does want United Methodism to have an industrial strength trinitarian theology at its core, and he insists on the canonical faith of United Methodism to drive this home.

We are now into the central elements in Bishop Jones's solution to the problem of division. Unity is to be achieved by a robust commitment to mission, discipline, and doctrine. The appeal to Wesley in his "Thoughts Upon Methodism" gives us a felicitous opening, even if it cleverly spins Wesley's words and ignores his moralistic diatribe about riches. Happily we can agree on the crucial significance of mission, discipline, and doctrine without signing on to the political blather about the extreme center. We need substance at this point, not geometrical slogans drawn from secular politics that disparage the alternatives before we start the conversation. So let's agree on the call to mission, discipline, and doctrine. We can cut each other slack on the best way to spell this out, but let's say that it involves making disciples, fixing society as best we can, relearning the spiritual disciplines, using the means of grace, and sensitively owning again the canonical doctrines of Methodism. Let's also agree on diversity in worship, language, ethnicity, adaptation to cultural conditions, and self-criticism all around. The bet, presumably, is this: work on all these challenges, and we will hold together and not divide.

Now this is an interesting bet! Yet we need to name the horses and check the racing form. "Schism, or splitting the Church, is an intentional decision to violate the discipline of the Church." This horse is conceptually shaky and empirically false. If canon law is in good shape, a church can readily survive violation (intentional or otherwise) of its discipline; the UMC has done so to date. However, let's try another horse: if the current position of *The Book of Discipline* on homosexual practice is significantly changed, then there will be an explicit split in The United Methodist Church. This is the horse that has to be watched.

All the others are not irrelevant, but they are secondary *where actual, current unity is concerned.* Thus we are not going to split over mission despite the intense internal dispute about this in theory and practice for thirty years. Nor are we going to amend the *Articles* on the Trinity, and drop, say, the *filioque* clause. Neither bishops nor members care enough about such an issue to get off the sofa. Nor are we going to ban college students from worship while they are in school. Nor are we going to split over race or gender or Scripture or Christology or the global nature of the Church. So slipping in that silly slogan about truth in theology lying in the extreme center is really irrelevant to the question of unity. At best this gives us a heuristic strategy for becoming slightly intellectually virtuous. We are not going to split over that, are we? Maybe Bishop Jones, like his great mentor of blessed memory, Albert Outler, is trying to impose on us his personal position on truth acquisition. Happily, that will not split us either, for we are illiterate and lazy as a Church on such technical philosophical issues.

So let's go back to the betting slip. The large print on the slip says there is a causal connection between discipline and unity. Suppose the small print says this: if the current position of *The Book of Discipline* on homosexual practice is significantly changed, then there will be an explicit split in The United Methodist Church. Are we ready to bet on this?

Of course we all know that there are differences on the morality of homosexual practice. There are also differences on the status of these options and on the warrants for them. Once these levels are run together, as they are here, it is crucial to keep our heads and see what is at stake.

There are wonderful moments of brilliant articulation that genuinely advance the discussion. Regrettably, I only have time for the problems. First, the third position is not the position of the UMC. Moreover, the exposition of it offered is wrong about the position on membership, and wrong to claim that the UMC is canonically committed to one standard for clergy and another for members. At the very least these propositions have to be supported and their consequences explored with great care. Second, Bishop Jones wants all persons holding to the three positions identified "to be included in our Church." There are critical equivocations here. Does Bishop Jones simply want people who *believe* all three positions to be members? Does he want all who *practice* all three positions to be members? Does he want the UMC to allow *canonically* all three positions? It is not easy to tell what he is endorsing. Thus he does say that if we change our canon law, there will be schism. And he insists he is a compatibilist, where compatibilism is the platitude that there can be different beliefs and opinions. (A full reading of "In Search of Unity" shows compatibilism to be the nontrivial claim that there can be different opinions *and practices* with respect to homosexuality.) We need clarity here. Without this we are not addressing cleanly the actual, impending, acute challenge to unity that we face once again at General Conference.

The critical question is this: Would a significant change in the canonical practices of the Church on homosexuality lead to division? I think it would. Good intentions are not enough at this point; we need appropriate circumspection. I am constantly astonished that those committed to change on this front do not see that they will divide the Church, just as they are now doing at such incredible cost in the Anglican Communion. The stakes are very high; Bishop Jones is right that division is a real danger. He is also right that work in mission, on doctrine, and on theology is vital to the welfare of the Church; he is even more right that canon law is critical to sustaining unity and avoiding division. However, it is the significant change of canon law on the practice of homosexuality that will precipitate division. It is this contentious matter that requires sustained attention.

I am sure that the pressure up ahead will be to speak much of compromise. No doubt we will hear from many quarters that we have gone round and round long enough on the issue of homosexuality; it is time to find a middle way and to move on in mission. The obvious compromise is to split the difference by not permitting homosexual practice for clergy but allowing it in the case of membership. I do not know if Bishop Jones is indirectly proposing this or not, but there are hints that he might be happy with such a way forward.

What should we make of this irenically intended move? First, the current position is already a way of compromise. Many local churches and their clergy already have adopted this position as a matter of practice on the issue of membership. There is clearly great pressure to make it the norm; so much so that one bishop acted with intemperate aggression against one elder who refused to go along. Only the work of the Judicial Council saved the day; and even then many bishops are still livid about its rulings. Second, should we take the next step and canonically endorse this proposal, we can well envisage gay and lesbian activists showing up at targeted churches to push their agenda by embarrassing those clergy who disagree with them. There will be a high political and pastoral price to pay up ahead. Third, this move would undermine the current teaching of the UMC that homosexual practice is incompatible with Christian teaching. As everybody knows (and Wesley himself taught) actions speak louder than words. So we can say good-bye to the official teaching of the Church. Once that goes, then a change on ordination standards will follow.

However, there are deeper theological issues at stake. It is not just a matter of empty promises of peace in the Church or of long-term consequences for ordination, this proposal would also involve four other crucial theological moves. First, it would set up a distinction between clergy and members that cannot be sustained. Of course, there will be differences between standards for clergy and members. We require that clergy be able to preach, for example. However, to set up radically different *moral* standards is odd in the extreme. Second, this proposal would also call into question the availability of sanctifying grace for all members of the Church. Somehow clergy have a pipeline to a deeper strain of grace than the rest of the Church; laity have to wait until they get to the other side. This is surely unthinkable for a church that was born as a holiness movement and that takes seriously Wesley's teaching on grace. Third, it would reflect a clericalism that puts ordination logically ahead of baptism in our vision of the Church. The clergy are the first-class Christians; laity can get in with the luggage. On the contrary, the conditions for baptism are logically primary; ordination takes place on the other side of the covenant of baptism. Fourth, and most important, the implications for baptism and Christian initiation are staggering. This move would make moral considerations secondary in the life of faith. United Methodism would have a lucky-dip conception of what is at stake morally in being a disciple. This would put us totally at odds with the standards of early Methodism, which made refraining from doing evil a condition of membership for its societies. It would also saddle us with a bizarre theology of baptism and Christian initiation.

The preliminary conclusion to be drawn is obvious: the proposal to split the difference on homosexuality is not some splendid middle way that will preserve the unity of the Church; it is a recipe for further turmoil and division in the UMC.

Lonnie D. Brooks

In his essay, "God's Gift of Unity for United Methodism," Bishop Jones has given the Church his own gift, and I am certainly grateful for his leadership in this matter, as I have been for some time on many others. Most United Methodists who have been involved in the connection beyond the local church know that it was his vision of the unifying nature of commitment to mission that led to the Church's adoption of the mission statement at the General Conference of 1996. Now our mission statement rolls as easily off the tongue as if it had always been there: "The mission of the Church is to make disciples of Jesus Christ." So it is fitting that Bishop Jones refers to a lack of agreement on mission as one of the two just causes of separation of the Church, the other being doctrine.

It is considerably easier, I think, for us to come to agreement on the nature of our mission, however, than it is on what our doctrine ought to be, especially if we are given some latitude, as we are, in how we define who is a disciple and what discipleship means. The real rub, then, is doctrine.

Bishop Jones has identified four levels of doctrinal sources of authority within the UMC. They are (1) Scripture, (2) constitutional standards, (3) acts and works of General Conference such as *Book of Discipline*, Social Principles, and *The Book of Resolutions*, and (4) liturgy and hymnody. Within category 2, Bishop Jones identified five standards, as follows: (a) the Articles of Religion, (b) the Confession of Faith, (c) the General Rules, (d) Wesley's Sermons, and (e) Wesley's New Testament Notes. I am bold to suggest that within this category he calls "constitutionally protected standards" there is an important hierarchy on which Bishop Jones might have profitably put more emphasis.

To begin with, not all the standards he puts in this category are constitutionally protected. In Judicial Council Decision 358 (JCD 358) the Council decided several important questions. It reaffirmed prior decisions that theological decisions were the purview of the General Conference, not of the Council, and specifically stated that the reference to Wesley's Sermons and Wesley's Notes as doctrinal standards was not a new standard of doctrine as adopted by the General Conference, since the language of neither the Articles of Religion nor the Confession of Faith was changed by that action. That essentially said that as long as the language of those two standards is not changed, it is the General Conference alone that decides whether or not any new standard of doctrine violates the first Restrictive Rule, which says, "The General Conference shall not revoke, alter, or change our Articles of Religion or establish any new standards or rules of doctrine contrary to our present existing and established standards of doctrine" (¶17). Just as important, JCD 358 established that Part II of the *Book of Discipline* in which reference is made to Wesley's Sermons and Wesley's Notes as doctrinal standards is not part of the UM Constitution. It is that reference by which Wesley's Sermons and Wesley's Notes are made doctrinal standards, meaning that by a majority vote of General Conference they can be rejected as doctrinal standards. That puts them in a much lower position on the hierarchy of standards than the first three.

But not even the first three are on the same level. The Articles of Religion (the Articles) and the Confession of Faith (the Confession) together are in a category of protection that is unique in UM polity. The Articles and the Confession are subject respectively to the first and second Restrictive Rules. Changing either standard requires a two-step process in which General Conference must first remove the Restrictive Rule by proposing an amendment to that part of the Constitution by at least a two-thirds majority, then at least three-fourths of the members of the annual conferences voting in the aggregate must affirm General Conference's action. Then, if that obstacle is overcome, General Conference must propose the desired change in either the Articles or the Confession.

The General Rules, while subject to the fifth Restrictive Rule, are not given the same level of protection as the Articles of Religion or the Confession of Faith. To change the General Rules requires the same two-step process as for changing the Articles and the Confession, but no three-fourths supermajority of the members of the annual conferences is required. The normal constitutional amendment process of two-thirds is all that is required for the removal of the fifth Restrictive Rule guarding the General Rules.

Bishop Jones has proposed parts of the Articles, the Confession, and, in another work, the General Rules as in need of some changes. I support that proposal, but I acknowledge that making changes will be tremendously difficult, if not impossible, particularly in the Articles and the Confession. Bishop Jones identified the vitriolic anti-Catholic articles as some of those ripe for change. My personal favorite is Article V of the Articles, which says the following:

> The Holy Scripture containeth all things necessary to salvation; so that whatsoever is not read therein, nor may be proved thereby, is not to be required of any man that it should be believed as an article of faith, or be thought requisite or necessary to salvation. In the name of the Holy Scripture we do understand those canonical books of the Old and New Testament of whose authority was never any doubt in the Church. The names of the canonical books are:
>
> Genesis, Exodus, Leviticus, Numbers, Deuteronomy, Joshua, Judges, Ruth, The First Book of Samuel, The Second Book of Samuel, The First Book of Kings, The Second Book of Kings, The First Book of Chronicles, The Second Book of Chronicles, The Book of Ezra, The Book of Nehemiah, The Book of Esther, The Book of Job, The Psalms, The Proverbs, Ecclesiastes or the Preacher, Cantica or Songs of Solomon, Four Prophets the Greater, Twelve Prophets the Less.
>
> All the books of the New Testament, as they are commonly received, we do receive and account canonical. (p. 60)

It is this article, among other things, on which our commitment to Scripture as the first doctrinal standard is established in our Church law. So this article is at ground zero in our discussion of doctrinal standards. The sentence that ought to be the focus of some considerable discussion, in my judgment, which goes right to the heart of the debate about the degree to which Scripture is an unambiguous standard of doctrine, is the one that says, "In the name of the Holy Scripture we do understand those canonical books of the Old and New Testament of whose authority was never any doubt in the church." There are many of the books included within the canon identified in this article whose authority we now know was disputed within the church from the very beginning. The example of

Second Peter comes quickly to mind, but there are plenty of others. Revelation and James are two such, and Luther himself called James "a book of straw."

It is rare for any serious work of theology to be a runaway best seller, but recently *Misquoting Jesus* by Bart D. Erhman achieved that status. Huge numbers of Christians and non-Christians alike now know that there is a lot of loose sand in the firm foundation of Scripture for doctrine in the Church. Nothing in Erhman's book is new, and for seminarians, in fact, it is all old hat. But we have not done a good job in bringing this kind of understanding about our canon to the laity, and I think such an understanding can make all the difference in how we treat the primary source of teaching authority in the Church.

Bishop Jones identifies six issues on which "our diversity might be compatible with our commitment to unity." They are race and gender, Scripture, Christology, homosexuality, global nature, and gift of unity and holy communion. I will not comment on all of those, but I do want to make what I think is an important observation on his statement that "In many ways, The United Methodist Church is a global Church." I think we might be a bit too full of ourselves when we make that claim and compare ourselves to the Catholic Church. The UMC has no members in South America, the Caribbean, Australia, China, India, Japan, Korea, or the Middle East. We have a pitifully small number in Central America. Even on our home continent of North America, we have no members in Mexico or Canada, restricting ourselves to presence only in the United States. We cannot make ourselves be global simply by saying we are. I think it is time for us to find another way to live into the call for being in global ministry than to try to stretch the UMC into having membership throughout the world. Perhaps it is time for us to look seriously at the World Methodist Council as the right vehicle for Methodists to be in ministry to the global community, which, in my judgment, will require that we work to restructure that body to be more open in its processes of leadership selection and financial accountability.

Finally, if I had composed the list of issues on which our unity is blessed by our diversity, I would have included the issue of pacifism and just war doctrine. Increasingly much of our professional leadership, and in particular the General Board of Church and Society, is pressing the Church to become a pacifist body aligned with the historic peace churches like the Friends and the Mennonites. Currently our Social Principles call us to the extreme center, condemning war as "incompatible with the teachings and example of Christ" (¶165C) and at the same time saying, "As Christians we are aware that neither the way of military action, nor the way of inaction is always righteous before God" (¶164I), and that war may "be employed only as a last resort in the prevention of such evils as genocide, brutal suppression of human rights, and unprovoked international aggression" (¶165C).

This issue of war and pacifism is one that I think has more potential to divide our Church than any other of the hot-button issues that are before us. I hope that at the upcoming General Conference we reject any effort to make the UMC a pacifist body.

MARY BROOKE CASAD

I'm grateful to Bishop Jones for this opportunity to participate in a "holy conversation" about the gift of unity for The United Methodist Church. I agree that our time and context yearns more than ever for a unified witness to the world, and that Christ as the Head of the Church bids us to be one body.

I also stand in the extreme center, understanding that the extreme center can exist only if all sides are given voice. I believe this is a strength of United Methodism, but it is often viewed as a threat to our unity. Therefore, I would offer the following three practices for us to consider as a way of living into the gift of unity:

Focus on Our Mission

The mission of the Church is to make disciples of Jesus Christ. If we agree that this is the work we are to be about, as Jesus commissioned us, and that we understand there is a process for forming and nurturing persons into deeper discipleship, shouldn't we be able to use this as our guide?

I would propose that we center our consideration of legislation at General Conference, and all of our actions at our various meetings and conference sessions around the question: "How is this action supporting our mission of making disciples of Jesus Christ for the transformation of the world?"

The criteria for answering this question could be "The Process for Carrying Out Our Mission" as outlined in *The Book of Discipline*, ¶122:

> We make disciples as we:
> —proclaim the gospel, seek, welcome and gather persons into the body of Christ;
> —lead persons to commit their lives to God through baptism by water and the spirit and profession of faith in Jesus Christ;

—nurture persons in Christian living through worship, the sacraments, spiritual disciplines, and other means of grace, such as Wesley's Christian conferencing;

—send persons into the world to live lovingly and justly as servants of Christ by healing the sick, feeding the hungry, caring for the stranger, freeing the oppressed, being and becoming a compassionate, caring presence, and working to develop social structures that are consistent with the gospel; and

—continue the mission of seeking, welcoming and gathering persons into the community of the body of Christ.

What would happen if we agreed to only consider legislation at the 2008 General Conference that supported our mission of making disciples as stated above? No doubt there would be various interpretations as to what constitutes disciple-making legislation, but at least we would be focused on our mission!

Certainly, the Seven Vision Pathways and Four Calls to Action and Areas of Collaboration that have emerged from the conversations between the Council of Bishops and the Connectional Table point us in a shared mission focus. As we seek to live the United Methodist way, start new churches, reach and care for children, and work to eradicate malaria and HIV-AIDS, we pull together toward a common goal. Let's focus on the difference we can make together instead of our differences!

Claim Membership in a Worldwide Church

When we take the vows of membership, we join The United Methodist Church and pledge a vow of loyalty. While our membership is placed in a particular local church, it is understood that we are connected to all United Methodist local churches. Could we help our members understand anew what it means to belong to a worldwide, "connectional" Church?

The "small world" stories within our connection excite and inspire us, giving us a sense of God's spirit vibrantly at work. Through global travel and communication, through Volunteers in Mission and special mission projects that pair local churches together from diverse places, to many ministries of various languages within our own conferences, we have opportunities like never before to understand Christ's command to "make disciples of all nations." Individual friendships that are formed frequently blossom into lifelong relationships with our Christian brothers and sisters, crossing all kinds of boundaries.

As Bishop Jones has stated, our United Methodist connection is uniquely poised to become a truly worldwide Church, instead of an American Church with mission outposts in other countries. As a part of our call to live the United Methodist way, could we seek out new opportunities to share the gift of our connectional Church with both members and nonmembers? Could we consistently proclaim from the pulpit and through teaching opportunities such as confirmation, membership and Sunday school classes that we are members of a worldwide Church with thousands of mission outposts (local churches) across the globe? Could we seek to provide more "hands-on" mission opportunities that link churches and people, thus helping them to grasp and claim the richness of our connection? Could we creatively use technology, such as our UMC.org community, to help persons thousands of miles away from each other in totally different cultural contexts feel connected to one another? Could we embrace our collective system of giving with a new enthusiasm and understanding, taking pride in the mission we are able to accomplish together?

Understanding that our myriad of members and ministries are "unique but united" helps move us closer not only to our United Methodist family but to the entire Christian family as well. Certainly world-changing disciples need to claim their identity as members of a worldwide Church!

Re-envision the Process We Use to Proclaim the Nonessential Doctrines of the Church

Dr. William B. Lawrence, Dean of the Perkins School of Theology at Southern Methodist University, speaking at a district training event in the North Texas Conference, cited the Rabbinical Assembly, the

Worldwide Association of Conservative/Masorti Rabbis. He noted their use of a particular process designed to reflect diverse views within the Conservative movement, which represents two million Jews worldwide.

Citing a press release from December 2006,[1] he told of a recent meeting of The Committee on Jewish Law and Standards of the Rabbinical Assembly on the subject of Homosexuality and Halakhah (Jewish Law). The committee serves in an advisory capacity, not as a judiciary body. The rabbis, synagogues, and institutions of the Conservative movement are guided by the boundaries set by this committee, but the committee uses a method to determine the parameters that allow for variations of practice, all recognized as legitimate viewpoints for the Jewish faith.

This method is described on the Rabbinical Assembly website (www.rabbinicalassembly.org):

> The Committee on Jewish Law and Standards sets halakhic policy for Rabbinical Assembly rabbis and for the Conservative movement as a whole. Its membership consists of twenty-five rabbis who are voting-members, as well as five non-voting lay representatives of the United Synagogue and one non-voting cantor representing the Cantors' Assembly. The Committee discusses all questions of Jewish law that are posed by members of the Rabbinical Assembly or arms of the Conservative movement. When a question is placed on the agenda, individual members of the Committee will write teshuvot (responsa) which are discussed by the relevant subcommittees, and are then heard by the Committee, usually at two separate meetings. Papers are approved when a vote is taken with six or more members voting in favor of the paper. Approved teshuvot represent official halakhic positions of the Conservative movement. Rabbis have the authority, though, as *marei d'atra*, to consider the Committee's positions but make their own decisions as conditions warrant. Members of the Committee can also submit concurring or dissenting opinions that are attached to a decision, but do not carry official status.[2]

As Dean Lawrence noted, the particular meeting on Homosexuality and Halakhah affirmed three teshuvots (responses). Each offered differing views, yet were affirmed as legitimately held views within Conservative Judaism. What united the committee making the decision was its concern for the unity of the Conservative movement worldwide.

Could United Methodists learn something from our Jewish brothers and sisters, he wondered aloud?

Bishop Jones stated that he does not regard the teaching on homosexuality as an essential doctrine. Would United Methodists be able to reach a consensus on what constitutes nonessential doctrines? Would we then be willing to create a process for the deliberation of nonessential doctrines, citing positions that received a certain percentage of votes as a valid expression of our faith community? Would this help us claim the gift of unity or make it harder for the extreme center to hold? For those united in concern for the unity of The United Methodist Church worldwide, it might be a worthwhile option to explore.

The gift of unity, like all of God's gifts, requires us to be good stewards of the gift in order to receive it fully. It requires our intentional efforts and special care. In gratitude for this great gift, it is my prayer that by living into the gift of unity, we may honor the Giver by more closely reflecting the heart and mind of the Giver. May it be so!

Amy DeLong

I remember the day *unity* became a dirty word to me. I was at the North Central Jurisdictional Conference in 2000. As with most jurisdictional conferences, there was time set aside for delegates and others to gather in forums with episcopal candidates. Each candidate had the opportunity to share a little about him or herself and then answer questions from the audience. At the first forum I attended, the candidate immediately began talking about Church unity. It was clear that keeping the Church together was of utmost importance to him. During the question and answer time, someone asked him how he intended to achieve unity. He answered, "We need to lift up those things we agree on, and de-emphasize our differences." The words of this episcopal aspirant scared me because I know that it is a short leap from "de-emphasizing our differences" to de-emphasizing *people* who are different.

Interestingly, this same candidate said that he was so against homosexuality that if The United Methodist Church ever changed its official position, he would consider leaving. Ten minutes after proclaiming that "unity was his top priority," he admitted that if things changed in a way disagreeable to him, he would leave.

My deep fear that day was that *unity* would become a code word, language used to lull the masses into complacency and to squelch conversation, dissent and debate—much the same way that the word *patriotism* was misused after 9/11.

In 2003, Bishop Jack Tuell preached a sermon entitled, "How I Changed My Mind," in which he recalled the story about how "fidelity in marriage and celibacy in singleness" became part of *The Book of Discipline*. Bishop Tuell said, "It is February 1983, a little over 20 years ago. I am meeting in an airport in Albuquerque with two other United Methodist bishops and an executive of the Division of Ordained Ministry out of Nashville. We are doing preliminary work on legislation for the 1984 General Conference; our subject matter was ordained ministry. We worked on many aspects of the subject. But a particular concern being raised was: How do we screen out homosexual persons from becoming ordained ministers? I proposed a seven-word addition to the list of things to which candidates for ministry must commit: Fidelity in marriage and celibacy in singleness. You would think that on as important a matter as that we might look to Wesley's guidelines of discernment: that is Scripture, tradition, experience, and reason. But I'm here to tell you that we did not look at the Scriptures; we never mentioned tradition; we did not refer to experience and reason. Instead of those four classic words guiding our conversation, we were unconsciously guided by two other words: *institutional protection.*[3] "Fidelity in marriage and celibacy in singleness" was nothing more than a linguistic slight-of-hand, a process to target gay people without looking like they were targeting gay people. This appeal for unity strikes me as the same kind of verbal manipulation—a way of protecting the institution by sacrificing faithful lesbian, gay, bisexual, and transgendered (LGBT) Christians.

One of my concerns about offering an essay in this book is that my participation will be seen as approval of its content. It is not. There is much I could take issue with in Scott Jones's writing (e.g., his beliefs about Christian superiority; his idolatrous view of doctrine; his failure to accurately recollect that the call for "amicable separation" at the 2004 General Conference was presented solely by the Good News Movement and was in no way a coordinated effort with progressives; and his depiction that the serious struggles toward racial and gender equality have been reduced now to primarily a "personnel" issue). However, my response will focus entirely on his few pages about homosexuality.

I have been doing spiritual direction with a client I will call Linda. Linda and her partner, Claire, were members of a conservative congregation that frequently preached and taught against homosexuality. Linda and Claire are faithful Christians in a committed, monogamous, long-term relationship—but their church judged them to be sinners and launched a campaign of spiritual torture against them. They were subjected to scorn, to threats of expulsion and eternal damnation if they did not renounce their homosexuality, and to reparative therapy (a model of therapy that claims to be able to change a person's orientation from homosexual to heterosexual, but that has been repeatedly discredited as destructive by the American Medical Association, the American Psychiatric Association, and the American Psychological Association).

Linda and Claire were forced to recite, "Homosexuality is a sin," over and over and over until they "believed it in their hearts." Linda and Claire were insistent, however, that homosexuality was not a sin and that the beauty of their love was a sign of God's blessing. But the pastor, his wife, and members of the church persisted in badgering them, even insisting they undergo a demonic exorcism. Eventually, Linda was driven to the brink of despair. Her spirit broken, she got into her car with the intention of committing suicide. Instead, she ended up at church where she went inside to pray. While praying, she fell into a deep sleep and when she awoke she says she heard the voice of God. "Linda, I love you. Go home." So she did, bearing the deep wounds of a church that almost killed her because of who she loves.

According to the status quo or "extreme centrist" position that Scott Jones exemplifies, Linda and Claire should keep going to church and resign themselves to harm, and those who have tormented them should continue to do so under the pretense of providing "moral clarity." And the Church will condone this pattern of mistreatment, calling it UNITY.

"Let's just keep the Church together," without regard for the most vulnerable among us, is a perversion of true unity and a toxic mandate reminiscent of an abusive family system that protects the abusers by requiring the abused to suppress their pain, tolerate the violence they experience, and deny their truth. Unity should never trump justice—but it does, and no place more glaringly than in the Church.

Put simply, I find Scott Jones's writing to be a dangerous combination of arrogance and ignorance. His superficial analysis reveals how unacquainted he is with the intricacies of this struggle, with the deep love and loyalty LGBT people have for our Church, with the immeasurable contributions we have made, and with the injustices we have suffered at its hands. In his *Letter from a Birmingham Jail*, Dr. King wrote, "Shallow understanding from people of good will is more frustrating than absolute misunderstanding from people of ill will. Lukewarm acceptance is much more bewildering than outright rejection."

The centrist position, maintained by Jones and countless others, is detrimental to true unity because:

- it continues the process of talking about LGBT people, rather than talking with us. The "don't ask, don't tell" policy of the UMC strangles genuine and truthful dialogue—and renders gay people and the real concerns of our lives invisible;
- it never challenges the injustice that inherently exists when the heterosexual majority passes legislation that excludes, oppresses, and restricts the rights of the largely unrepresented homosexual minority.
- it perpetuates the myth that "Nothing in Scripture supports same-gender sexual relationships and many key texts condemn it." If one does even a cursory review of Scripture, one will find only a few texts that refer to homosexuality (none of which are "key") and a slightly deeper analysis will clearly reveal that these references do not resemble in any way what modern people understand as adult, mutual, loving same-gender relationships;
- it implies that homosexuality is a sin, when it is not;
- and, it suggests that no self-avowed practicing homosexuals are serving as clergy. Surely Scott Jones and every other U.S. bishop knows a gay or lesbian member of the clergy—and many regard these people as some of the most effective and faithful pastors in their annual conferences.

Unity will never be achieved in the presence of silence and in the absence of truth.

I believe the position that Jones represents is detrimental to true unity because it erroneously claims that The United Methodist Church's current disciplinary statement "allows for the Church to be in ministry with gay, lesbian, bisexual, and transgender persons without proclaiming that their behaviors are compatible with Christian teaching." This is just a more cumbersome way of restating one of the oldest and most hurtful anti-gay sentiments, "Love the sinner, hate the sin." I cannot name one gay person, not one, who feels "loved" when this sentence is inflicted upon us. It is hatred couched in the language of love for the sole purpose of enabling the one speaking these words to feel both sanctimonious and guiltless when saying them. In her book, *The Grace of Coming Home*, Melanie Morrison says:

> How can you say that you love me . . . when you don't want to know either my pain or my joy? No, I don't think you can say that you love me, because what you call "sin" (the love I share with April), I call a grace-filled relationship, and what you call your inability to condone, I call the sin of heterosexism. There's a serious rupture between us, and we can't gloss it over with easy talk about loving the sinner while hating the sin. For you to call the most intimate and cherished relationship in my life "sinful" is a very serious charge. It's a violent thing to say. Furthermore, you can't offer me love with one hand while denying me justice with the other, because love and justice are inseparable. No, I'm sorry, I won't grant your wish to think that you can love me anyway.[4]

Distinguishing between homosexuality and homosexual practice creates spiritual schizophrenics. It divides our flesh from our spirit, the truth we know from the truth we tell, our being from our doing. How vile to tell me that my sexual orientation is not the problem, the problem is that I love someone. **Unity will never be achieved in the presence of spiritual violence.**

The opinions expressed in Jones's writing are detrimental to true unity because they sanction discrimination and prejudice. Throughout his piece, Jones says in various places,

"God is love."

"It is all about love of God and love of neighbor. We can be absolutely right, but if we have not love, we are nothing."

"God created all people in God's image, regardless of skin color, language, ethnicity, or whatever. All persons are precious in God's sight."

"One of the sinful tendencies of human beings is to seek to limit who God is."

"By valuing diversity of all kinds, we can affirm that God is big enough to welcome everyone."

Appealing to our sameness in God's sight, to our universal blessedness, and to God's expansive love, Jones invites us to let go of the human constructs that divide us. He rightly identifies sexism and racism as "sin that plagues American culture and infects the life of the Church." (Although he fails to mention that this was once a revolutionary notion that contradicted the deeply held "extreme centrist" position that women and people of color were not fully human, and that it often takes a radical view of justice to form and inform an ethical center.) But then, rather than continue in this same spirit, Jones instead asserts that the Church's practices and policies of overt discrimination against homosexuals are defensible. Jones abandons his scripturally grounded beliefs about inclusiveness and equality in order to justify the Church's intolerance and duplicity—and in so doing creates back-of-the-bus Christians and mocks the gospel of Jesus Christ. **Unity will never be achieved when bigotry is disguised as intellectual debate**.

It is deeply disingenuous to assert that "we can continue with our current teaching without schism." We are already torn apart. Every day gay and lesbian people are subjected to brutality and harsh judgments, to contempt cloaked in righteousness, to rejection, ridicule, and recrimination—and that's just at Church.

SUDARSHANA DEVADHAR

Bishop Scott Jones, in his attempt to find the "extreme center" in maintaining and celebrating the unity of the Church, offers valid and compelling points to prove his thesis. In his essay, Bishop Jones clearly articulates the biblical, historical, missional, theological, ecclesiological and doctrinal foundations that call for such unity. According to Jones, the need to address certain questions is important, for example, "Who is God? What must we do to be saved, that is in a right relationship with God? What is the way of salvation?" In his analysis, Bishop Jones identifies some gifts of the Church in the areas of diversity, of worship, language, and ethnicity. These gifts are essential in establishing unity. Clearly not denying the pains of racism, xenophobia, and sexism that torment the fabric of unity, Bishop Jones calls the Church to claim its Wesleyan roots in healing and finding harmony. Bishop Jones's prophetic claim is clearly and convincingly conveyed: "The United Methodist Church should not split. Nor should its leaders allow it to be torn apart. Nor should anyone let herself or himself so focus on one part of the Church's life or mission that the gospel beauty and excellence of the whole is ruined." He is passionate in his discussion of the only two legitimate reasons John Wesley would have endorsed the splitting of the Church: "if the Church teaches doctrines that are contrary to the essential doctrines of the faith, and if the Church prevents you from being in mission to persons whom God requires you to reach." In responding to his essay it would be very difficult to disagree with Bishop Jones, given his credible and persuasive arguments.

I would like to enter into dialogue with Bishop Jones so this debate could be deepened and strengthened. Perhaps the best way to start is by asking the very question Bishop Jones ends his book with when he asks the Church to wrestle with the question of, "How do we live more fully into this gift of unity?"

Undoubtedly, Bishop Jones has laid a strong foundation and elaborated very clearly the necessity to live this question from all angles, namely the angles of Scripture, history, mission, theology, ecclesiology, and doctrine. However, he either has not dealt with some of the issues that we need to struggle with to strengthen and deepen the unity of the Church or has not mentioned them. In order to use more fully this gift of unity, I believe we need to get into deeper dialogue on a few issues that hang as clouds over our deliberations.

First and foremost among them is our whole approach to the Wesleyan Quadrilateral. Bishop Jones identifies it well when he says, "The extreme center position is to affirm that the Bible alone is our authority, but it is never alone. It should be interpreted with reason, tradition, and experience, properly employed." While I agree with him 100 percent, let me also hasten to identify the problem that is being faced by our Church in this arena. Even before we learn how to interpret the Scripture with reason, tradition, and experience properly employed, most of the time we do not try to interpret the Scripture with integrity. In our interpretation of Scripture, we tend to be historical and literal on some matters, and cultural and contextual on others. Unfortunately, most of the time we do this based on convenience. Is this right? Should we use the Scriptures to advance our own theological agendas, or should we use integrity in advancing the reign of God on this earth?

Second, as a global Church how do we learn to live together as partners in Christ, free from direct or indirect expressions of imperialism? To put it more bluntly, can we continue repeating the same mistakes we have made in the expansion of missions in the nineteenth century? One of the major mistakes the Church made in its propagation of the gospel in the nineteenth century was converting others to the Christian faith by giving them wheat or rice. Church historians have referred to them as "Wheat Christians" or "Rice Christians." Many times people accepted Christ as their Lord and Savior not because of the content of the gospel but because of how the gospel was packaged, i.e., along with material gifts of rice or wheat! Some of the people who became Christians through this method might not have really demonstrated their light for Christ in their Christian witness. The records of the missionaries who used this method of evangelism might have looked impressive at the time to their respective mission boards that sent them from North America and Europe. However, the question one should look into is how effective these churches are today in their Christian witness. The lesson we need to learn from this is that we cannot repeat the same mistake in the twenty-first century. In this instance I am not referring so much to the arena of evangelism but to how we do our holy conferencing! One cannot live in unity until our General, jurisdictional, and annual conferences become holy and bold conferences! One of the things that I believe might help our General Conference become a holy and bold conference is by doing away with complimentary breakfasts, lunches, and dinners around caucus and special interest groups. When delegates come from different economic backgrounds, when their expenses are paid for on a per diem basis, particularly at a time when a good percentage of the global population lives under one dollar a day, saving money makes a big difference! However, with the cultural diversity of our Church, sometimes the offer of free food elicits feelings of obligation or misunderstanding on the parts of different global communities. This alone may hinder the goal of unity in the Church, particularly when someone has to participate in a holy conferencing with obligations tied to our style of hospitality including free breakfasts, lunches, and dinners. In moments like this, our Christian hospitality, however well-intended, may become unholy in the midst of our holy conferencing.

Third, I heartily agree with Bishop Jones when he refers to the "essential elements of Christian unity: mission, discipline, and doctrine." I also want to concur with his comment about our holistic process of making disciples, quoting from *The Book of Discipline*:

> The Process of Carrying Out Our Mission—We make disciples as we:
> —proclaim the gospel, seek, welcome and gather persons into the body of Christ;
> —lead persons to commit their lives to God through baptism by water and the spirit and profession of faith in Jesus Christ;
> —nurture persons in Christian living through worship, the sacraments, spiritual disciplines, and other means of grace, such as Wesley's Christian conferencing;

—send persons into the world to live lovingly and justly as servants of Christ by healing the sick, feeding the hungry, caring for the stranger, freeing the oppressed, being and becoming a compassionate, caring presence, and working to develop social structures that are consistent with the gospel; and

—continue the mission of seeking, welcoming and gathering persons into the community of the body of Christ. (*Book of Discipline*, ¶122)

One of my former colleagues in the Greater New Jersey Annual Conference Cabinet, Rev. Dr. Lloyd Preston Terrell, always helped us talk about difficult issues around the Cabinet table with candor and integrity. Whenever he raised a point that was difficult to talk about, he always started his sentence by saying, "Now you need to love me." Let me say to my readers that you need to love me because I ask the following question out of my love of the Church: "What percentage of our resolutions at the General Conference help us to make disciples for Jesus Christ?" We talk about making disciples for Christ for the transformation of the world but set our priorities based upon the membership model. In my opinion, when we give importance to numbers instead of the holistic process of disciple-making, we hinder the unity of the Church instead of strengthening it. In my heart and mind, I believe that unless we are committed to changing from a membership syndrome to discipleship syndrome in holy conferencing we will not see progress in our goal. Perhaps one way of addressing this issue is by giving preference to equal numbers of delegates from each region of our denomination instead of numerical representation based upon membership. Additionally, in the best interest of the Church, we need to seat delegates not by area but randomly so that there is more time to get to know one another across the denomination. In this way, there will be a true and meaningful Holy Conferencing, placing aside feelings of regionalism. In my opinion, addressing these practical issues around how to hold holy conferencing may contribute to helping us become serious about getting involved in the holistic process of disciple-making.

Finally, our call to "spread scriptural holiness across the land (globe)" is perhaps more urgent than at any other time in our history. We are standing as Christians with Wesleyan rootings in a world where the blessings and curses of globalism are standing side by side and at times working against one another. These challenges are evident not only in the rich countries of the world but also in the poor countries. In a situation like this we are called to be the Church to make a difference in the world. We cannot afford to be a global Church if we are not willing to be united in our Christian discipleship in addressing and fighting against all kinds of evils that are present in our world. As a delegate to the last two General Conferences, one of my frustrations is that as a global Church we cannot universalize our theological issues and sociological issues. A theological issue in one part of the globe may be a sociological issue in another part. In our struggles to find uniformity on these issues, we may fail in addressing some of the deeper issues such as the impact of poverty, illiteracy, racism, war, sexism, and xenophobism, which are tearing apart and ruining our humanity and increasing our separation from the realm of God.

SALLY DYCK

If ever it would have seemed that things were falling apart, the center couldn't hold, "mere anarchy loosed upon the world," "the ceremony of innocence . . . drowned; / "the best [lacked] conviction, while the worst [were] full of passionate intensity" (from William Butler Yeats's "The Second Coming," which Bishop Scott Jones uses to describe his perspective on the "extreme center"), it would have been the night in which Jesus was betrayed by his own disciples.

In Luke's account of the Last Supper (22:24-27), a dispute broke out among the disciples as to who would be regarded as the greatest. Jesus tells his disciples in the midst of the dispute that there are many models of power and authority in which some "lord" it over others, **"but not so with you"** (Luke 22:26a, emphasis mine). Jesus makes clear that within the Christian community, we are commanded to deal with disputes according to a model of power and authority that is different from that practiced in the world around us.

While nation-states divide and civil wars ensue, let it not be so with us. While we may have disputed and divided before, let it not be so with us now. We are not to reflect the power dynamics of the world around us, but to pursue another way. I hope that other way is in the United Methodist way.

Unity Is the Christian Task of Peacemaking

Bishop Jones says that unity is a gift of God that needs to be "received rather than achieved." Theologically, a gift is something that is given freely, requiring nothing but a willingness to receive it. Grace is the ultimate gift that God gives us. While we have a response-ability to this gift, we do not work to obtain or achieve it.

Jones rightly suggests that how we view unity—as a gift, a command, or a promise—determines our approach to it. In Jones's comments and the Scriptures he cites, the verbs are telling: unity requires *working* together, *searching, continuing* conversation, *praying* much, *making* every effort, *studying, looking* for signs of God at work, and more. Quite frankly, unity demands constant work!

A gift entailing that much work is like receiving a vacuum cleaner for a birthday present! It's a gift that's meant to be put to work in order to have meaning. I fear that if we approach unity only as a gift and not as our task, it will be like a treat given to several children—we will haggle over whose it is and/or how to cut it.

Therefore unity, in addition to being a gift of God, is our Christian task—the work we have as a Christian community. Further, the Holy Spirit empowers us and works through us to live in unity. Unless we consider unity to be an imperative and our task, we may view it as optional. It is through unity that we fulfill the Church's mission to make disciples of Jesus Christ and transform the world.

Unity is entwined with both functions of the mission: making disciples and transforming the world. In order to make disciples in the midst of dispute and to transform a disputing world, we must make peacemaking an essential activity, skill, and commitment. Just as a dispute arose at the Last Supper, even in Christian community we can't avoid it. However, we can learn how to live in unity in the midst of disagreement.

Jesus said, "Blessed are the peacemakers, for they shall be called children of God" (Matthew 5:9). Yet peacemaking is vastly misunderstood in both society and the Church. Peacemaking is not passive, as many believe, but intensely active—at its best, proactive—in providing tools and skills to help us be "salt and light" as we live in Christian community with all the diversities that Jones describes.

Peacemaking is fundamental to discipleship, specifically to disciple-making. Conflict is a major contributor to numerical and spiritual decline in congregations. No one wants to be a part of a community that is in unhealthy and constant conflict. To equip Christians to make disciples is to equip them to make true peace, bringing healing and reconciliation where there has been long-standing hurt and brokenness. We do not have to be perfect or all agree within the Church. That would be uniformity, and nowhere does Scripture or Christian tradition speak of uniformity as our task or goal. However, when we live in peace and unity, we move our mission forward.

My bold dream for The United Methodist Church is that we equip local churches to be workshops of peacemaking discipleship. The congregation is not the only entity in our culture that needs the skills of peacemaking. Families need to learn how to talk through their differences to avoid divorce and estrangement. Co-workers, employers, and employees who have increased skills in working through differences would experience greater productivity. Because annual conferences, General Conference, and our general boards and agencies are called to resource local churches for making disciples, their task needs to include equipping the saints for peacemaking discipleship.

A part of peacemaking is the way we communicate with each other about our differences. In the discussion about United Methodist unity, words such as *schism, split, separation,* and even *amicable separation* are bandied about without thoughtful consideration of their implications. The level of pain in the midst of our disputes is high. Some desire simply to eliminate the pain by sending the disagreeing parties their separate ways. Going our separate ways does not guarantee to lessen pain; nor does it remotely offer healing. As Jones says, the United Methodist DNA is not over doctrinal dispute; if we go our separate ways, we will all carry ecclesiological DNA from our unresolved disputes.

A decision to split doesn't mean one side goes one way and the other goes another. When I was young, my mother acquired some CorningWare dishes, a new product that could be put in the oven or freezer without breaking. These took a lot of heavy daily use as they withstood the normal wear and tear our family gave them.

One day I was carrying a dish down into the cellar, which had a concrete floor, and I accidentally dropped it. It broke, but it didn't crack in two. It totally shattered to the point that there were hardly any pieces big enough for me to pick up with my fingers. I discovered that CorningWare is held together by tension. It takes a hard blow to break the tension; but when it does, it shatters and splinters the dish into tiny little pieces.

When people contemplate whether The United Methodist Church

should split, it's not as simple as thinking one side will take half the plate and the other side will take the other half. What about all those congregations in our connection whose members have a diversity of theological perspectives? Certainly, tensions exist within congregations about the key issues described by Jones. But without their congregation—even a congregation with people who disagree with them—many people will give up on the Church altogether. Some will never seek another worshiping community. People who want to remain part of their congregation won't know which one of its many different "sides" to take, if forced to choose. Families will struggle too, as they embody all the diversity within the larger Church. If we try to force a break in tension, The United Methodist Church would splinter or shatter into many pieces, not split into just two.

If, as Jones states, the denomination was "preoccupied" with the merger of the Methodist and the Evangelical United Brethren churches, our preoccupation with separation will derail any focus or momentum toward our mission. This would be the worst result of all. Furthermore, the world—including its nation-states, families, and other daily contexts of disagreement—will never know another way: the "not so with you" way of being and making disciples of Jesus Christ.

Unity is more than a gift; it's an imperative with an urgency and skill set that we disciples must embrace for the fulfillment of our mission. We're given the imperatives of peacemaking discipleship: "clothe yourselves with compassion, kindness, humility, meekness, and patience. Bear with one another and, if anyone has a complaint against another, forgive each other. . . . [C]lothe yourselves with love, which binds everything together in perfect harmony. . . . And be thankful" (Colossians 3:12-15).

I want to thank Bishop Jones for the opportunity to be in dialogue with him. Before serving on the Council of Bishops together, we had our disagreements over the issues that threaten the unity of the Church. However, we resolved early on to make it "not so with us." Through our growing understanding of what has shaped the differences in each other's lives, through dialogue about them and also affection, I wholeheartedly join him in affirming an unswerving commitment to the mission and the unity of The United Methodist Church.

95

JAMES A. HARNISH

Can the center—even an "extreme center"—hold?

I share Bishop Jones's appreciation for William Butler Yeats's image of the falcon drifting in a wider and wider circle because it cannot hear the falconer. It may be a painfully accurate description of our denomination.

As a delegate to every General Conference since 1980, I have seen "the best lack all conviction, while the worst are full of passionate intensity." After the 1996 General Conference in Denver, I re-read the history of the separation in 1844. I was pretty well convinced that we were headed in the same direction. Again in Cleveland there was a particularly painful moment when if felt as if some of the folk with "passionate intensity" were ready to tear the connection apart.

A decade after Denver, I see some signs of hope that we will once again find our center and become a living movement of the Spirit. Leaders like Scott Jones are one of those signs. Vibrant local congregations that are clear about their mission and are ministering to their communities are another. The empirical evidence, however, indicates that we may continue the slow hemorrhaging of members, congregations, ministry, and resources that Lyle Schaller described in *The Ice Cube Is Melting*[5] until there is little left to hold us together other than the pension fund.

I share Bishop Jones's conviction about the "doctrine, spirit, and discipline" of the Wesleyan tradition. I am convinced that when we share the faith out of the center of our spiritual and theological tradition, masses of spiritually searching people will respond, "Where have you been all my life? This is exactly what I've been looking for!" The unanswered question is whether The United Methodist Church will practice "the Stockdale principle," break out of its institutional denial, and become the Spirit-energized movement through which that Wesleyan witness will be shared effectively in the twenty-first century.

As I read the essay I entered into debate with Bishop Jones as to whether unity is a gift (something we already have by God's grace), a goal (the vision of the kingdom of God into which we are called to live), or the result (the by-product of commitment to the extreme center he describes). While all three are important, I lean toward the third, namely that the New Testament vision of unity is the result of a common commitment. Unity is what happens when faithful disciples are bound together in the "doctrine, spirit and discipline" and are energized by the Spirit to fulfill the mission of making disciples for Jesus Christ.

My perspective is shaped by my experience. I never expected to be involved in a congregational schism, but then I was appointed to Hyde Park Church. The full story is told in the book *You Only Have to Die*,[6] but the short version is that I found a century-old church that had a very strong sense of its past, was foggy about its present, and didn't have a clue about what God was calling it to be in the future.

During the arduous process of defining our theological identity and congregational mission, we discovered that when the center is unclear, folk tend to hang together under the illusion that the Church is what they believe it to be while engaging in skirmishes about borderline issues. But when people define what is at the center, some folk will rise up and cheer while others rise up and walk away. It was a painful and costly experience. But out of that process of dying, new life was born. Since we defined what is in the center—the gospel, the Creed, our history, mission, and core values—we have been able to live (for the most part) with gracious respect for differing convictions about things on the circumference—worship styles, politics, even homosexuality.

I seriously doubt that talking about unity would have moved us into the future together. But when we focused on our mission, we discovered a center than continues to hold. As long as we are united at the center, we can handle some measure of diversity around the circumference.

Three challenges confront this center-circumference approach. First, not everyone can live with clarity at the center and diversity on the circumference. Some people need absolute clarity the whole way around. To change the metaphor, some folk are fly fishermen who need to know that every fish they catch is a trout. Others are like the anglers in Jesus' parable who drag a big net across the bottom of the sea, gathering "all kinds" and allowing the sorting out to come at the end. My sense is that only big-net anglers are comfortable with the vision of unity and diversity that Bishop Jones describes.

The second challenge lies in the fundamental difference between a congregation and a denomination. As a congregation, we can wrestle with circumference issues while sharing personal relationships in Christian community. Hopefully, the deeper the relationships and the stronger the sense of community, the more diversity we can handle. General Conferences are not primarily about relationships, but about discipline. They are not about building community, but about establishing boundaries. The very nature of the General Conference tends to separate people on the circumference rather than pulling them together at the center. This is particularly difficult for a connectional denomination in which decisions at the General Conference impact the entire system in contrast to a congregational system that allows for more autonomy in its different parts.

The other side of this challenge is the growing gap between the General Conference and the local church. There sometimes seems to be an inverse relationship between the vitality of a local congregation and that congregation's connection to the bishops, boards, and agencies. This disconnection significantly complicates any expression of unity that is defined from the top down.

If, as Schaller would say, we expect next year to be 1955, we could expect expressions of unity at General Conference to be effective in resolving tensions and drawing our congregations together in a common mission. But since the next General Conference will meet in 2008, we can probably anticipate continuing growth of the congregation-and-denomination gap. It may be that similar to the way Bishop Jones describes restructuring the global Church, we will eventually need to consider some way to share a common core identity while giving more autonomy to annual conferences and congregations.

The third challenge rests in the way American Methodism has historically reflected the American culture. Bishop Jones effectively describes the "make or break" issues within the denomination, but he does not deal with the way the polarizing tensions in our Church are often a mirror image of the political polarization of our culture. The passionate intensity of the folk on the extreme right and left is as tedious as it is unrelenting. Given the profound need for biblical and theological training that Bishop Jones describes, it is very difficult to move people away from their political or cultural assumptions into genuine dialogue that grows out of a biblical and theological center. The falcon continues its gyre, unable to hear the falconer.

I believe that the unity of the Church is ultimately a spiritual issue and that a lack of unity bears witness to a lack of what Jeremiah called "a fire in the bones." While there are notable exceptions, in far too many places we are afflicted with a spiritual aridity for which the only antidote is a renewal of spiritual life that is rooted in "the doctrine, spirit, and discipline" and energized by a fresh movement of the Holy Spirit.

Will the center hold? I certainly hope so! Any schism along the lines of the current denominational debates would leave those of us at the center with no place to go. I pray that the "extreme center" will not only hold, but that it will thrive and become the core of our witness to the world. While Mr. Wesley's fear of our becoming a "dead sect, having the form of religion without the power" has already become a tragic reality in far too many places, I pray that we will discover what it means to "hold fast to both the doctrine, spirit, and discipline with which [we] first set out," thereby overcoming our fear and giving hope to the future.

CAROLYN E. JOHNSON

The timeliness of the volume and the method in which Bishop Jones addresses, interrogates, and answers a challenging array of issues is refreshing and provocative. The semantic intrigue of *extreme center* invigorates the discussion on unity. Each topic is arguably an important component in the discourse on unity; however, I will confine my contributions to the intersections of racism, diversity, and the global nature of the Church.

There is a perception among many that the Church's intense debates on homosexuality have diverted significant Church-wide attention from other important and difficult discussions including racism. The polarization fueling these debates has seemingly positioned homosexuality as *the* singular threat to our shared life. Bishop Jones's recognition of racism as a critical factor affecting Church unity is an important reminder of our historic commitment to racial justice and the Church's unfinished agenda.

Eradicating racism is demanding, complicated work! As a denomination, our efforts to reduce prejudices and stereotypes, eliminate discriminatory practices, examine power relationships, and achieve equity in resource utilization have had considerable success. Yet, racism continues.

Bishop Jones's placement of racism as a doctrinal issue offers both invitation and analytical space to discuss this difficult topic. At the extreme center, it offers an opportunity to reinvigorate the character of our disciplined life—the voluntary willingness to be responsible for and obligated to one another.

Participants were asked in a racism workshop to eat a piece of candy given them by the facilitator. Puzzled, because candy wasn't on the table or in their packets, participants couldn't comply. A few, to humor the leader, mimicked eating "pretend" candy. Undaunted, the leader reminded the group of her history of honesty and trustworthiness. She challenged them to act as though they **really** believed either in her or in her words. Several rifled through papers; some looked around their chairs;

and a few entered the task with energetic seriousness. They decided if she said it was so, then it must be so! One of those students looked under the table and also turned his chair over. To his amazement, and that of the entire group, candy had been taped under each chair. As leader, I reminded the group the candy was placed in anticipation of their need and was there **before** they were there. The intensity of their actions was in direct proportion to their ability to believe. Actions based on the limits of a skeptic's belief will not yield answers to difficult challenges. Are we endangering the integrity of our witness and our capacity to offer solutions for ourselves and our communities? Is a skeptic's point of view adjusting our belief system to disclaim the power of Christ "to make all things possible"?

Breaking Fellowship—The Silent Schism

Are we in danger of breaking fellowship due to frustrations and resentments on the unfinished agenda on racism? Antiracism work can be simultaneously rewarding and draining, especially given the evolving complexity of racism. Many give up! Bishop Jones discussing the "Church as a means of grace" reminds us "part of the Church's witness should be the visible display of that peace and love within its life as an institution and among its various members individually." Yet, across the racial spectrum, and with increasing frequency, commentary illustrative of giving up includes *"Haven't we worked on this long enough?" "Why do we have to keep teaching this again and again, can't they get it?" "What more are we supposed to do?" "They don't really want to change." "Isn't this reverse discrimination?" "When is it going to be our turn?" "Why do we get left out?" "Have they really repented?" "Have they really forgiven?" "Things can't really change." "It's time for someone else to do this work."*

We may agree racism is sin, but is there the broad-based sense of urgency compelling us, with renewed vigor, to examine racism in its varying dimensions. How do we restore the importance of this work? We continue to create groups of opposites such as:

- those who contend we haven't gone fast or far enough and those who assert we've become too race conscious and, as such, perpetuate reverse discrimination and political correctness;
- those who view most situations through a racialized prism and those who claim not to see race at all; and
- those reluctant to discuss racism for fear any "honest" engagement will result in being labeled racist or race traitor and those who believe "honest engagement" is impossible due to institutional ambivalence and apathy regarding racial justice.

In the midst of unsolved racism, are we settling for silent cohabitation as a replacement for genuine community? Are we creating a *virtual* internal schism, landscaped by our frustrations and resentments?

If hearts give up on each other, have we "broken the fellowship" and failed to understand the importance of the gift of unity?

Racism's Evolving Complexity

The development of "coherent answers" necessitates understanding racism as a complex global phenomenon and requires a powerful Christian witness to combat the ambiguities, contentions, and transgressions it generates. Racism in its most horrendous forms are easily recognizable, genocide and ethnic cleansing for example. Racism in our institutional structures is decidedly more subtle. Current scholarship, most notably the work on aversive racism and unintentional bias by Gaertner and Dovidio[7] provides insight on how people who subscribe to egalitarian values are able to perpetuate racism.

Globally, the Church is faced with racism both in regional contexts and with some common themes worldwide. For example, in a U.S. context, a black-white dichotomy is no longer analytically sufficient to examine the increasing intricacy of racism and pluralism of our congregations and communities.

Throughout the worldwide connection we should explore

- how our racial/ethnic/and national legacies impact our identity, witness, and understanding of Christian community;
- how our Christian beliefs shape, if at all, our racial, ethnic, and national identities;
- how our resources, programmatic emphases, and governance structures align with the diverse needs of our congregations and members;
- how we bear one another's burden, especially in responding to racism.

Diversity and the Extreme Center

Left or right, conservative or liberal, directionality exists only in relation to the center. As place, the extreme center has dimensions, energy, and, for a connectional people, the important elements of shared vision and memory. As process, the extreme center incorporates a praxis of inclusion. Our capacity for effective witness grows as we deepen our understandings about the nature of God. As a storied people, the diversity of God's working in our lives provides a rich curricular base for learning.

A balanced centrist position avoids the tendency to reduce diversity to a litany of categorical labels and doesn't confuse or substitute gateway and pipeline inclusion strategies as accomplishment endpoints. Differences are not perceived as deficits, and critical thinking and inquiry are essential. We engage each other understanding that no single group is the exclusive repository of knowledge, insight, analysis, creativity, or intellectual capacity; therefore, we learn *from* each other and learn *with* each other. We are not competitors. Further, the intrinsic value of inclusion to shaping a centrist position enables us to tackle difficult issues and respond to situational imperatives with solutions that are creative and innovative; enables us to resolve problems and brokenness in ways that are healing and therapeutic; and provides us with an effective witness to the world, based on the integrity of our beliefs and actions—or demonstrating that our rhetoric and record are one. A tightrope performer understands the physics of center mass to perform dangerous feats without falling. We depend on the centrality of Christ—the center that propels us forward with courage, confidence, and caring for a hurting world.

I love The United Methodist Church and treasure the gift of unity, not only because of who we are, but who we can be!

By language, race, and nationality I was an outsider. But walking in the door of Kwang Lim Methodist Church in Korea, I was at home. The barrier of language was removed by participation in the rituals I knew so well. The choir, singing in Korean, performed a medley of spirituals from the African American tradition. Tearful eyes were everywhere; we were one, connected by a shared sense of victory over sorrow. For those present, we were as one—gifted, each in our way to know "his eye is on the sparrow" and personally comforted by "and I know he watches me." If we remain steadfast in our belief and tenacious in our efforts, together, we can face any problem. This is the gift of unity. To God be the glory.

SUSAN J. LAURIE

It would seem unnecessary to need a position paper on unity within our United Methodist Church. However, Bishop Jones recognizes the stress on our Church today. As Jones advocates for an understanding of diversity and inclusion and their importance to mission and evangelism, I feel some hope. He writes, "The world needs as many concrete expressions of diverse unity and reconciled diversity as possible. It needs a united Church. It does not need Christian churches dividing, splintering, or fracturing" (p. 10). I agree.

As a United Methodist who is also a lesbian woman, I believe with Bishop Jones that the debate on homosexuality is a symptom of a deeper disagreement. However, I also know that leaders who would fracture our Church continually scapegoat gay people as the cause. It is common, but unfair, for anyone to suggest that the maneuvers for an "amicable separation" at the 2004 General Conference were anything but an exercise by the Good News United Methodists.[8] For gay and lesbian people, being separated from our church homes never feels "amicable." I agree with Jones that splitting the Church is ugly business. It is schism and against our understanding of God's hope for unity among Christians.

I am grateful for the people called Reconciling United Methodists (RUMs) who advocate for the full inclusion of people of all sexual orientations and gender identities. At the 2004 General Conference, Reconciling Ministries offered a theme of "Watermarked: A Ministry of Assurance" that called upon people to trust in their baptismal covenants. *We are permanently and powerfully part of the family!* was our mantra. RUMs hope to remain part of an intact UMC. We understand that the dramatic moments of the General Conferences are nothing compared to the long four years in between GCs when we find ourselves without a Church home. We want to be inside serving and worshiping Jesus Christ.

My hope is continually fed by my upbringing in Sunday school. When I was a child, I was the beneficiary of the efforts of Sunday school teachers, choir directors, and pastors whose lessons and hopes for us children were grounded in Jesus Christ. I did not know at first that I was gay, nor was I burdened by the harsh treatment that would come later. I learned many stories and songs about God and God's love for me.

One lesson that comes to mind in the ecclesial discussion of this book is one that involved hands. "Here is the church, here is the steeple. Open the doors! See all the people." We learned that the "church" is not the building, but the people. We learned what parables were and how Jesus surprised people by teaching new ways to love and serve God. Jesus was warned to be more prudent by some of the disciples, but he kept on widening the circle and treating "others" as equals in the kingdom. You can name them as well as I can—Samaritans, lepers, and women. I felt loved in my local church. I still believe with a child's heart that *"Jesus loves the little children, all the children of the world."* The diversity of those children was another point of that song.

I appreciate Bishop Jones's argument for diversity in our denomination. The history of prejudice and exclusion of whole categories of people is a tragic tradition of the people called Methodist. It is good that we now see how the Scripture and words of Wesley work together to overcome the residual prejudices against people of color and women in our Church culture. Paul writes and Bishop Jones quotes, "As many of you as were baptized into Christ have clothed yourselves with Christ. There is no longer Jew or Greek, there is no longer slave or free, there is no longer male and female; for all of you are one in Christ Jesus" (Galatians 3:27-28).

However, he fails to follow the logic of his own argument into this generation's debate on who can be included. It was painful to read the words of Bishop Jones (words such as: *all, fully human, diversity, unity,* and *inclusion*) that supposedly characterized the catholicity or inclusivity of the Church knowing that they were only meant for nongay people. We are all human beings, created in God's image, with a capacity to love others.

As Jones notes, there is diversity in God's creation. Sexual orientation is one of the diversities within humankind. Even our *Book of Discipline* supports my identity when it proclaims,

> We recognize that sexuality is God's good gift to all persons. We believe persons may be fully human only when that gift is acknowl-

edged and affirmed by themselves, the church, and society. (*Book of Discipline*, ¶161G)

In this brief essay, I hope to be clear. Homosexuality is not a sin. Maybe we did not know it in 1972 when antigay language was first written into *The Book of Discipline*, but we know it now. Homosexuality is not a sin and neither is the forming of loving families by people who are gay or lesbian. We know gay and lesbian people who are wonderful life partners to each other, loving parents to their children, and esteemed members of communities, faculties, and local churches.

Jones asserts that his analysis of "Six Key Issues" are logically patterned and that there is a "balanced, centrist position" for Christian response to key issues (p. 52). Then his application to issues of race and gender are inclusive, but his proposal for homosexuality diverges from all that he has argued, to leave the abusive policies in place. Surely, he must realize that "all" necessarily includes me as a lesbian woman. I am a human being. Human diversity includes gay people. "Unity" requires inclusion. "Inclusion" requires acceptance and welcome. Jones does not see my humanity.

The unity Jones proposes with a double standard for the participation of gay and lesbian people is a false unity. Like the racism before it, it assumes an innate superiority of the majority class. It was very interesting to me that he acknowledges the formation of the racially segregated Central Jurisdiction, noting, "It is significant that no African American delegate to the 1939 General Conference voted for the union because of this segregation" (p. 52). Obvious to the African Americans, the "union" proposed was a false unity.

Our UM *Book of Discipline* needs to be changed to reflect our understanding of God's love for all people. To faithfully continue the logic of Bishop Jones's study and writing would be to argue for change—to advocate the full participation of gay and lesbian United Methodists. The disjointed suggestion by Bishop Jones to leave it the same is an old idea that has not brought unity.

United Methodists were at the same place in 1991 when each annual conference was charged to vote on the language of *The Book of Discipline*. In my home conference, Western Pennsylvania, a young man, an ordained deacon described as very gifted and "one of our own," was defrocked for being a "self-avowed practicing homosexual." This added to the tension as we focused on the ordination ban. When the petition urged the General Conference to keep the antigay prohibitive language the same, a daring amendment was proposed. In it Reverend Maurine Waun suggested the addition "while realizing the need to remain open to the Holy Spirit, which continues to inform our understanding and interpretation in this matter." The Holy Spirit was voted down by a 90-10 percent landslide.[9]

None of the past votes that relegate gay and lesbian people to a segregated reality have brought unity. The only thing holding us back, threatening our unity as a Church, is prejudice and the efforts of some to encode prejudice into law. It is emotion that causes us to betray our own logic, betray our understanding of the presence of God in our time, betray the young man and his calling, and hold stubbornly to misconceptions.

The contempt that lies within a plea to keep the current dehumanizing language about homosexual people is harmful to our United Methodist Church. While some strive to make this "compatibilist"[10] approach seem harmless, the targets of the discrimination are laid open to the inherent abuse. This solution appeals only to those who refuse to really see or listen to their own Church family members. Their "polite" disregard turns quickly to agitation when gay or lesbian Christians ask to be treated equally.

As understanding about sexual orientation has grown, there is hope that we can move into an inclusive era with some grace. Unity requires integrity. An integrated body of Christ will not proscribe a segregated tier for our gay and lesbian family members. Integrity requires truth.

I have participated in the Reconciling witnesses of the last three General Conferences. Our themes of hospitality (1996), open communion (2000), and baptismal covenant (2004) have positively communicated our hopes for an inclusive UMC. Each time, delegates have come to our Reconciling United Methodists and confessed, "I am on your side, but I voted against homosexuality because I was afraid." Sometimes they say they are afraid the Church will split. Some are afraid of others in their own delegation who are watching them vote. I do not ask people to act against their conscience, but if the Holy Spirit has convicted them on what is right, then they need to speak and act for that truth.

In our struggle for full inclusion, even our friends fall into the trap of compatibilist moderate. They tell us to wait, to be more polite, to appreciate the crumbs from the table. We are not pets; we are human beings. While it is indeed nicer to be kept indoors, rather than outdoors, we will not be trained to stay away from the table. We are human beings, precious children of God, and responding to God's call in our lives. We are aware of treatment or words that diminish our participation in the full life of Christian community. Those who tell us to be patient are the ones who have a Church to go to. We are impatient because we do not have that comfort.

People who "believe" homosexuality is a sin have been misled. Wrong teaching about homosexuality will one day disappear with the old teaching against left-handedness. The phrase "the practice of homosexuality is incompatible with Christian teaching" needs to be flipped. It is not the homosexuality that must be eradicated, rather it is the "Christian teaching" that alienates gay and lesbian sisters and brothers that must be stopped. Reread Bishop Jones's essay and let every "All" mean "all." As in the children's play, "Here is the church, here is the steeple. Open the doors. See ALL the people."

This is not a complicated issue. Rather, it is a matter of breaking a bad habit of discrimination. We inherited a "belief" that homosexual people were morally different. Now we know that both heterosexual and homosexual people have the same gifts and graces and human frailties.

Perhaps our Church is at its best when we teach the children. Fortunately for me, I believed those early lessons in Sunday school, and they have informed how I understand the whole of the Christian message. For me, a thorough reading of the gospel of Jesus Christ was the salvation from self-hatred that antigay messages sought to implant. Through prayer and Scripture, I learned to trust God even more than I might have in an unexamined life. Thankfully, Christians in my life supported my participation in local church, and I continued to benefit from good teaching and shared worship.[11] I was not called "divisive" for wanting church.

One day the UMC will be fully welcoming of gay and lesbian people. Leaders who challenge and assist congregations into this future are the ones who truly value unity as God's gift to the Church.

As I wait for the day, I find comfort and strength in the words of Jesus, the Good Shepherd, "My sheep hear my voice. I know them, and they follow me. I give them eternal life, and they will never perish. No one will snatch them out of my hand" (John 10:27-28).

BILL MCALILLY

Offering Christ

Bobby rode his bicycle to Beauvoir United Methodist Church. Bobby knew to come on Tuesday because the food pantry would be open. He was graciously received and given enough food to last him several days. Climbing back on his bike, he tried to balance the sack of groceries on the handlebars as he rode off. Bobby is one of the many homeless people who wander into United Methodist churches daily in search of a meal. By providing physical nourishment for the hungry, Beauvoir is living the abundant life.

Tom is a twenty-four-year-old college graduate working in one of our denominational institutions asking hard questions about the mission and ministry of The United Methodist Church. He sees a Church with great potential but also one that has lost its focus. In a sense, Tom sees what the rest of us have been unable to see, unable to name. What he names is a Church that has forgotten its first love. "In our forgetting," says Tom, "we are pushed not toward unity but into isolation and struggle." Tom is seeking the abundant life. Will he find it in The United Methodist Church?

Janice is the mother of three. She is longing to find meaning in her life. She comes to her pastor with more questions than she has answers. She aches with an emptiness that keeps her from living with any real sense of peace. In conversations with her pastor, she begins to discover the presence of God right at the root of her emptiness. Janice begins to bridle the impulse of mechanical and exhausting human "doing" and begins living as an enthusiastic human "being." Jesus Christ moves beyond being an intellectual idea to being a living reality. Janice discovers the abundant life.

Notice each vignette begins, not with an agenda, but with a person. In order to achieve unity, United Methodist clergy and lay leadership must move to a renewed recognition: unity will come only as people like us offer Christ to people like these in a broken world.

Prayerfully aspiring for unity, our denominational conversation must be careful to attend real persons wrestling with real-life issues. The message the world receives every four years when The United Methodist Church is said to speak seems to be reactive to the hot button topics of the day rather than faithfully witnessing to the life-changing presence of Jesus Christ in the world.

Bishop Scott Jones faithfully names the dilemma and leads in a new direction. He offers a way forward with his work, "God's Gift of Unity for United Methodism." As I asserted at General Conference in 2004 during the unity debate, we must hold the tension of the opposites long enough until God reveals a solution. Jones correctly argues that holding the boundaries of our Church, as well as the tension, will bring us closer to God's vision for the kingdom of God than will schism. In the context of biblical theology, when the waters are stirred, the healing comes. The waters in all mainline denominations are stirred presenting United Methodists, beyond fear of crisis, opportunities to be healing agents in our time!

The greatest problems we face in The United Methodist Church are not human sexuality or doctrine. Our Wesleyan doctrine is sound and needs no correction. The underlying difficulty in our denominational membership's search to find unity is the dangerously divisive quest for power. In the recent past, many have strayed from the genius of Methodist "conferencing" to petition, lobby, and desire to control. Conversations about emerging priorities are being aborted. The sanctuary of mutual respect for unique gifts and diverse perspective is being tragically compromised. Rather than believe in a thriving future, our community focus has narrowed to a fear of further losses or even survival of our denomination.

The image of the extreme center, which Bishop Jones offers, will allow the Church to deal more effectively with the strains and struggles of power.

Instead of preoccupation with sinful power to create winners and losers, the Church is called to focus on the consolidating power of God. Of course, current issues are vitally important. Faithful people must continually wrestle to formulate spiritually discerned and painstakingly thoughtful, responsible stances on serious emerging issues.

The UMC must weigh every response, however, with a God-perspective, which we apprehend through the discipleship of Jesus and the continuing ministry of the Holy Spirit in our midst. We must never avoid dealing with social questions, but we also must never surrender the unique, transcendent perspective, which is the hope of Christian people.

Years of debate among General Conference delegates and the resultant ecclesiastical legislation have failed thus far to strengthen the Church in significant ways. Worse, media attention seems to accentuate what casual witnesses would view as internal bickering. All of this is a distraction from God's call in our lives individually and corporately. What are we proclaiming to the world about United Methodism, even Christianity, in these controversial moments? Mission doesn't make headlines. Love won't be mentioned. Grace and peace and forgiveness will be silent. The world needs a Savior—and we have him—and we are hiding him from those who need him.

The heartbreak many of us feel is a fear that unity is not possible. After the dust settled on May 7, 2004, it was finally recognized that there is a large, silent voice within The United Methodist Church that is not aligned with any one group. Voices urged us to become organized, to get a platform, to posit another position to counter those already in place. In truth, there is the temptation to politicize the desire to hold the Church together. However, at the end of the day, what is needed is not more political maneuvering. We do not need more people lining up on one side or the other. What is needed is for The United Methodist Church to be reminded of our focus and our mission. Bishop Jones calls us to that task effectively. When we gather for General Conference in 2008, we will represent persons, both lay and clergy, who daily live out this mission by faithfully proclaiming and demonstrating the gospel. These persons serve in soup kitchens and clothes closets. They go on mission trips both at home and to the far ends of the earth. They are bringing rejuvenation to the Gulf Coast Region in the aftermath of Hurricane Katrina by restoring hearts, homes, and churches. They teach Sunday school, sing in the choir, lead worship, and visit in prisons. In short, those we need to remember are the silent ones who have no agenda save offering Christ to a hurting world. The vision that will bring about unity begins in recognizing our need to be connected to one another in spite of and sometimes because of our differences as we, together, remember our call to make disciples.

In the end, I believe it will be churches like Beauvoir who model for us a way forward. It will mean establishing congregations that create a true sense of sanctuary where we risk ourselves in the greater world in the name of Christ. It will mean being a part of the Christian fellowship that understands its purpose to share the gospel and its life with others who are alone and estranged. Focusing on anything other than this vision for the kingdom will not lead to unity.

The last time I saw Tom he said to me, "I believe that we trust the boat more than we trust God and risk faith." At our best, this willingness to let go, to trust, and to risk is who we have been as United Methodists. It is what makes our life together meaningful and effective in ministry. Our life together is a sacred trust full of the messy as well as the miraculous. Our future together will depend on how well we can attend, appreciate, align, and attune ourselves to people and places of need. Only then will we discover that our unity does not come from legislation. Unity comes as a by-product of being faithful to Christ, through knowing one another as children of God, and finally, by loving others as Christ has loved us.

In the words of Jesus' prayer in John 17:21-23 "As you, Father, are in me and I am in you, may they also be in us . . . so that the *world* may know that you have sent me and have loved them even as you have loved me."

Patricia L. Miller

Bishop Scott Jones has done an excellent job in writing this essay. He has clearly articulated the issues facing The United Methodist Church. I am grateful to him for inviting me to contribute to this book. I am a United Methodist by choice. I love our triune God and his Church. I uphold our doctrinal standards and our Wesleyan tradition.

Throughout the essay Bishop Jones refers to finding the common ground in "the extreme center." Let's look to John Wesley to see what "the extreme center" is for Methodism in Wesley's explanation of what is a Methodist. John Wesley did not like the reproach used against him and his colleagues for their disciplined way of life. In fact, he said he would rejoice if the name Methodist might never be mentioned. Further, he said "if that cannot be, at least let those who will use it, know the meaning of the word they use"[12] and so he wrote the "Character of a Methodist." In the first paragraph in that document Wesley wrote:

> We believe, indeed, that 'all Scripture is given by the inspiration of God'; and herein are we distinguished from Jews, Turks, and infidels. We believe the written Word of God to be *the only and the sufficient* rule both of Christian faith and practice; and herein we are fundamentally distinguished from those of the Romish Church. We believe Christ to be the Eternal Supreme God; and herein are we distinguished from the Socinians and Arians. But as to all opinions which do not strike at the root of Christianity we 'think and let think.' So that whatsoever they are, whether right or wrong they are no 'distinguishing marks' of a Methodist.[13]

In this paragraph Wesley states one of the principles that makes Methodism so appealing to us. We can be and must be open-minded about matters that are not central to the Christian faith. There is to be latitude of belief within the Christian family. And we United Methodists are grateful for a heritage that calls us to focus on the great doctrines of the faith that the orthodox church has upheld for nearly 2000 years.

In this same paragraph Wesley writes about "the center" of the Christian faith. It is the absolute supremacy and uniqueness of Christ.

The supremacy of Christ was always central to Wesley and it must be to us.

Still in the same paragraph, Wesley makes it clear that there is a central, a foundational revelation that has made Christ known. He refers to it as "Scripture" and as "the written word of God." What's more, he describes the Scriptures as "the only and sufficient rule both of Christian faith and practice." No doubt, if that statement had been made by one of the leading members of the Confessing Movement it would be denounced as "extreme."

But what is "the extreme center"? If "the extreme center" is a commitment to the Wesleyan understanding of what is at the heart of our faith joined with a Wesleyan insistence that we listen to and learn from others, then true unity is possible.

Also central to Wesley was what he described as holiness of heart and life—praying without ceasing, doing good to all, and living our faith as Christ taught us. The Methodist

> as he has time, . . . 'does good unto all men'—unto neighbours, and strangers, friends, and enemies. And that in every possible kind; not only to their bodies, by 'feeding the hungry, clothing the naked, visiting those that are sick or in prison'; but much more does he labour to do good to their souls, as of the ability which God giveth: to awaken those that sleep in death; to bring those who are awakened to the atoning blood, that, 'being justified by FAITH' they may have peace with God, and to provoke those who have peace with God to abound more in love and in good works. And he is willing to 'spend and be spent herein', even to "be offered upon the sacrifice and service of their faith', so they may 'all come unto the measure of the stature of the fullness of Christ'.[14]

Conversations about unity need to start with the most basic truths of our faith. John Wesley called them "the common fundamental principles of Christianity—the plain, old Christianity that I teach."[15]

To arrive at a solution to our dysfunctional United Methodist family, discussion must begin with some common agreement and understanding about doctrine and discipline; otherwise, we are bound to fail. If there is agreement on the fundamentals of our faith, unity will follow.

When my father died in 1998, I had great comfort and peace because I knew his salvation was assured. That assurance is what I want not only for the people I love but for all people. All people should have the opportunity to hear the Word of God taught in truth. Our clergy are not called to preach their own ideas; they are called to preach and teach the gospel of Jesus Christ.

There is a belief in Christian circles that whenever people of faith disagree, they can solve the problem by compromising. It is assumed that if each side will just slide toward the other, they can agree on the lowest common denominator. While that approach may be effective in solving some problems, it is risky and, perhaps, even dangerous in matters of faith.

Jesus did not say, "Let's find some spiritual principles on which we can all agree." Indeed, Jesus was quite narrow and rather exclusive in saying, "I am the way, and the truth, and the life. No one comes to the Father except through me" (John 14:6).

Even though Christianity has a special relationship with Judaism, the apostles did not suggest that the two faiths work out a compromised "middle ground." Indeed, Peter declared, "There is salvation in no one else [but Jesus], for there is no other name under heaven given among mortals by which we must be saved" (Acts 4:12).

Ours is a revealed faith. We believe that God has given to us all necessary and essential truth in an inspired book. We regard the Bible as "our true rule and guide for faith and practice." The Christian church has given us the Apostles' and Nicene Creeds as summaries of the Bible's message, establishing proper boundaries for belief.

In our Methodist-Wesleyan tradition we are committed to the Articles of Religion, the Confession of Faith, Wesley's Standard Sermons, and his Notes on the New Testament. These doctrinal standards are essential in our identity and our unity.

Without a clear definition, the danger in seeking the "extreme center," as Bishop Jones advocates, is that we might become extremely mediocre and forfeit our birthright in the process. In the search for unity we must be faithful to the essential revealed truth of Scripture. We cannot compromise the truth.

The Confessing Movement within The United Methodist Church started in 1994. "[It] is a witness by United Methodist lay men and women, clergy, and congregations who pledge unequivocal and confident allegiance to the Lord Jesus Christ according to 'the faith which was once for all delivered to the saints' (Jude 3). The faith of which Jude wrote is the Church's faith, the apostolic faith. Not a human contrivance, this faith centers on Jesus Christ, fully God and fully man; and on His life, death, resurrection, ascension, and promised return as attested in Holy Scripture."[16]

From the very beginning, the Confessing Movement has supported unity within The United Methodist Church. On April 29, 1995, the Confessional Statement was adopted. A portion is as follows:

> In love for the Church we . . . now present this Confessional Statement for the renewal and reform of The United Methodist Church.
>
> The crisis before us is this: Will The United Methodist Church confess, and be unified by, the apostolic faith in Jesus Christ; or will The United Methodist Church challenge the primacy of Scripture and justify the acceptance of beliefs incompatible with our Articles of Religion and Confession of Faith?[17]

The Confessing Movement continues to support unity within The United Methodist Church. At the 2005 National Conference of The Confessing Movement, a statement on *Unity in Christ, That the World May Believe* was adopted. Portions of that document are as follows:

> Our official United Methodist teaching is more than adequately articulated in our Constitutional Standards. Proposals for unity that ignore, evade, or minimize our historic standards are inadequate. . . .

> False understandings of inclusivism demand acceptance apart from repentance and obedience to the good news of God's grace for all sinners. . . .

> Genuine unity, as a precious gift of the Holy Spirit, is rooted in the gospel of Jesus Christ, witnessed to in the Holy Scripture, summarized in the ecumenical creeds, celebrated in worship and sacraments, demonstrated in common mission, articulated in our teaching, lived out in love, and contended for by the faithful.

Recovering and sustaining unity requires:
- a new appreciation of the necessary role of official doctrine in the intellectual and spiritual life of our denomination,
- the careful teaching of the apostolic faith by bishops, pastors, and seminary professors, including its call for personal and social holiness,
- diligently maintaining the beliefs and standards of *The Book of Discipline* as a covenant of trust.

Practices that contribute to disunity include:
- neglect of Scripture and disobedience to our Doctrinal Standards,
- claims of new sources of revelation that set aside the authority of Holy Scripture and the tested moral standards of the church,
- capitulation to lifestyles that are inconsistent with Christian discipleship.

There is a new hunger for the stabilizing role of classic Christian teaching in our denomination. Dissent is inevitable and not to be feared. Principled dissent is to be tested in Christian conferencing by its congruence with Scripture and the church's Doctrinal Standards.[18]

In the essay, discussion of the schism experienced within the Episcopal Church is described by Bishop Jones. The Episcopal Church with internal conflict and severed relations to the World Anglican Church provides a lesson for The United Methodist Church relative to unity in doctrine.

Bishop Jones has raised many issues associated with unity within our denomination. Time and again he raises the issue of the authority of Scripture and doctrinal standards, and rightly so because they are the "extreme center." We are a part of a World Church. Will we find unity within The United Methodist Church that we might find unity with the worldwide church of Jesus Christ?

John Wesley got it right on theology, mission, and ministry. We would do well to follow his example. May we pray without ceasing that we may be faithful disciples of Jesus Christ and that the Holy Spirit will bring unity in the truth.

JOHN R. SCHOL

From the very beginning Christian unity has been elusive. Over the centuries, we have tragically severed the body of Christ countless times. The *World Christian Encyclopedia*[19] reports there are more than 33,000 Christian denominations.

Recently, Bishop Scott Jones, Bishop Sally Dyck, and I set out on a journey together to participate in divergent events such as the Confessing Movement's Convocation (advocating for The United Methodist present stance to not fully include homosexuals) and the Hearts on Fire Convocation (supporting the full inclusion of homosexuals) to learn more about the deep wounds and division within The United Methodist Church and the basis for true unity. I gained much from the experience and agree with Bishop Jones that it is incumbent upon all disciples not to further divide the body of Christ.

Yet, we as United Methodists find ourselves severely divided on several issues. Some have contemplated another schism. I applaud Bishop Jones for his commitment to find a basis for unity in the midst of our current struggles.

However, Scripture also suggests that division within the body of Christ can serve a purpose. Healthy faith communities do not inadvertently let their commitment to unity downplay differences and hinder it from being led by the Spirit to be more like the eschatological vision of God's heavenly banquet (Isaiah 25:6-9 and Luke 14:15-24).

What is the purpose of division within the body? In 1 Corinthians 11:17-22 Paul writes:

> Now in the following instructions I do not commend you, because when you come together it is not for the better but for the worse. For, to begin with, when you come together as a church, I hear that there are divisions among you; and to some extent I believe it. Indeed, there have to be factions among you, for only so will it become clear who among you are genuine. When you come together, it is not really to eat the Lord's supper. For when the time comes to eat, each of you goes ahead with your own supper, and one goes hungry and another becomes drunk.

What! Do you not have homes to eat and drink in? Or do you show contempt for the church of God and humiliate those who have nothing?

Scripture teaches that division and factions within the body of Christ
can be a means of discerning who among us is committed to *genuine* community, who is willing to surrender privilege for the sake of participating
together in the Lord's Supper and Christ-centered community.

The privileged (advantages and benefits attached to individuals
because of their status) are able to arrive at the supper table before
our poorer sisters and brothers because the poor need to work longer
hours. We who are privileged need to wait to eat rather than filling
ourselves and getting drunk while we wait for others. In other
words, division and factions can help us see how we use privilege to
divide Christ.

When division and factions expose our privilege, it is the responsibility of we who are privileged to examine how we are dividing the body of
Christ and to relinquish our privilege. This was Paul's understanding of
how division and factions could be helpful within the body.

The Corinthians experienced division not only at the Lord's Supper
but also because some Corinthians used the doctrine of the Holy Spirit
and their gifts for self-glorification rather than to build up and unify the
body of Christ (1 Corinthians 12).

Repentance, not schism, is the appropriate response to division.

The privileged find it hard to repent. We enjoy our privilege and refuse
to face it, choosing instead to theologize it, or find justification for it in
the Scriptures, or refuse to seek to understand what is obvious to those
over whom we have privilege. Schisms occur because we are blinded by
privilege. It is through Christ that we become aware of our privilege and
repent for the ways it separates us from God and one another.

Our challenge is that we cannot be so committed to the principle of
unity that we inadvertently stifle the division and factions that emerge
within the community to expose the privilege of some over others. To do
so would cut off opportunities for Christ to work within the community
and to invite repentance. The people who will be hurt by this the most
are the privileged themselves. Without the division and factions how will

they have the opportunity to see that their privilege is dividing the body of Christ, as happened in Corinth?

We sometimes are tempted to live as though scriptural interpretation and doctrine exist as objective and abstract entities separate from Christ. But without the experience of Christ and Christ-centered community (as experienced in the Lord's Supper), we cannot interpret Scripture or understand doctrine. Division and factions within the body should not cause us to resolve our differences by debating doctrine and scriptural interpretations. It should cause us to ask whether we are interpreting Scripture and understanding doctrine in light of Christ-centered community or whether privilege has caused us to read Scripture and understand doctrine to protect and reinforce our positions of privilege.

This has been our mistake in the past. We have interpreted Scripture and understood doctrine to protect such manifestations of privilege as denying ordination to women, permitting the owning of slaves, and legitimizing the colonization of other nations. Our interpretation of Scripture and understanding of doctrine is fallible and must be subject to the test of whether it is consistent with the biblical norm of Christ-centered community as manifested in the sharing at the Lord's Table. Division and factions can be ways of challenging and exposing the misuse of Scripture and doctrine to maintain the privilege of some over others.

Ultimately, doctrine is the servant of Christ. Christ is not reshaped to fit doctrine, but doctrine is reformed to the spirit of Christ. When interpretations of Scripture and understandings of doctrine are used to protect privilege, they become anti-Christ. When such interpretations and understandings are lifted up as boundaries to define who is in and who is out, they must be scrutinized to see if they are undermining Christ-centered community and the Lord's Supper. It is the interpretations of Scripture and understandings of doctrine that do away with privilege, which can form the center and boundaries of Christian community. Jesus talked about our relationships and judgment in the community as the first shall be last and the last shall be first and that to follow him we must become servants of all (Matthew 20:6; 21:31; Mark 9:35). In Jesus' teaching, doctrine became a tool of the privileged rather than providing

God-given boundaries. Community is not judged by doctrine, but instead the community manifested at the Lord's Supper judges, shapes, and applies doctrine.

The challenge is to manage division and factions in such a way that the privileged have every opportunity to repent of their privilege. The challenge is for the disadvantaged to stay within the body while persistently and lovingly articulating the pain of the hurt caused by the behavior and attitudes of the privileged.

We witnessed this kind of healthy, loving, creative tension when African Americans and women chose to stay within the Methodist Episcopal Church even when they were not granted the full equality and communion promised through the Lord's Supper. It was their presence and the division and factions eventually caused by the privilege of others that led to the beginnings of repentance within our Church and the possibility for us to understand that racism and sexism are inconsistent with our understanding of the doctrine of creation. Most privileged Christians did not understand the implications of the doctrine of creation for racism and sexism until they had to come to terms with the unequal treatment of African Americans and women within the Church.

Bishop Jones's proposal of an "extreme center" position on divisive matters is attractive. It avoids simplistic answers and slogans and recognizes that many divisive issues are complicated and difficult. It encourages good-willed discussion among thoughtful people. It articulates a way to stay together and to keep the peace.

The great risk, however, is that it will hinder those of us who benefit from privilege within society and who carry this assumption of privilege into the way we act in the body of Christ from having the opportunity to repent. We risk continuing to assume that the racial, gender, and global privilege we are used to in the world is acceptable within the Church as well.

It is not our understanding of doctrine but our repentance that transforms the world. The road to repentance is difficult, painful, and bitter; but it is the only route to healing and redemption.

Privilege, and the desire to safeguard it, corrupts all. In the Gospels, it is the privileged, especially the religious leaders and elites, on whom Jesus concentrates his call to repent (John 3:3).

Privilege requires us to reexamine all our assumptions. The need to repent of our privilege calls into question how we interpret Scripture, what we define as the essence of our doctrinal standards; which ones we assume to be essential and which ones we decide we can modify. Often the very things we are most convinced of are the ones that serve and protect our privilege the most.

Schism would be tragic. We must do everything possible to avoid schism. Theologizing and complicating the division and factions to prevent those of us who are privileged from the opportunity of seeing our need to repent is harmful.

When division and factions emerge, we need to stay together, listen to those who are hurting, and be willing to explore our own motivation and repent. This is radical, and it is not always the center. It will more often be found on the margins as John Wesley and Jesus experienced and taught.

JOE M. WHITTEMORE

What indebtedness I feel to Bishop Jones for taking a risk at an extremely critical juncture in the life of our Church. I commend him for his straight talk and courage in not trying to please the masses and sound good. His application of biblical teachings is extremely helpful. There is clearly integrity in his work.

I am sincerely in awe of Bishop Jones's invitation to write this response. As a CPA and not a theologian (by choice), this review must be from a practical laity perspective. Unless I fail to represent my peers well, I should make no apology for this viewpoint since 9,739,000 of the 9,794,000 members of The United Methodist Church are laity.

Bishop Jones's observations evoke my sincere appreciation. His reasoning and insights are right on target. Using his account of Wesley's teachings, there is little questioning that our current differences come very close to justifying separation. We are talking about more than simply disagreeing on issues that can divide the Church. Unless we can live together in mutual covenant, our mission will be shortchanged. For the Church to visibly display peace, it must have peace.

Diversity of race, language, ethnicity, gender, and age are great strengths. Diversity on whether Jesus is the only way or whether Scripture is primary divides us and causes distrust. It's not the presence of different people that is killing our mission. The danger is in radically different theological beliefs. Simply, the edification of believers is not the acceptance of contrary doctrine. I hope and pray for the continuation of the UMC but have grown tired of the maneuvering, the constant bickering, and the prejudice against orthodox, conservative thought that can be found throughout our general Church leadership.

I love the Bishop's comments on "different positions all within the boundaries of the playing field" and "there being defining limits to the Church beyond which one can be said to have left the denomination." Major questions for United Methodists today, lay and clergy, include: (1) "What is the playing field?" and (2) "What are the rules we are going to play by?" We are currently confused. If throwing a baseball from the catcher to the left fielder constitutes a score, how does a person holding a tennis racket score on the football field? Sounds ridiculous, but clarity is lacking! Diversity that causes apprehension, confusion, and mistrust is not a virtue and is probably not a gift of God.

Are we confusing the matter of Christian unity with denominational community? Mission rather than unity must be our goal. By asserting that division is a hindrance to the Church of Jesus Christ, are we claiming that the Church would be stronger today if all we had was the Roman Catholic Church? As Wesley suggested, there can be union in affection without entire external union—one heart, though not one opinion.

Bishop Jones points correctly to the stresses and strains on our unity increasing over the last several decades. We do not have clearly held common values. Our mission is suffering, and we are not reaching the potential of ten million Christians. To succeed in carrying out mission, the members of any group must work in concert with one another.

Bishop Jones is very wise to accept, honor, and celebrate that there are different sides in our Church. I believe the three expressions in the UMC as identified by the Bishop are one seeking what is best for God's Church and the two exterior sides adamantly believing their convictions. I contend our strife is not about dominating others' beliefs, but about being able to freely and dramatically support our own beliefs.

Is our conflict about more than homosexuality? I believe the answer is clearly yes. Are the real issues essential doctrine? Again I believe the answer is yes. Our Church must be more than back and forth, never-ending war. We must focus on other priorities than the endless discussion of homosexuality.

Diversity that causes deep division and constant discord will always divert mission, cause mistrust, foster lack of togetherness, and turn the focus away from ministry. I am not sure whether we have "forgotten" our mission or become indifferent to it. Laity will not listen to complicated theological bickering without losing interest. We need to understand to be motivated. When one Bishop supports the beliefs stated in the

Apostles' Creed and another calls those same beliefs into question, we laity lose interest. We do not commit well to double messages.

Bishop Jones "nails" one of our great weaknesses when he reminds us that "persons called to the ministry of an elder are not called to preach their own theology." Bishop Jones places too much emphasis on local congregations being social clubs and too little emphasis on the past forty years of seminary teachings. Too often, local churches are not social clubs, rather they are bully pulpits for every different belief conjured by modern clergy. This weakness might improve over time if seminaries had to earn laypersons' money rather than abducting it through the arbitrary splitting of Ministerial Education Fund dollars between "approved" seminaries. Laity have an interest in supporting the training of our future pastors, not in sustaining the faculty as an institution.

One of the fundamental mistakes we are making in the UMC is thinking of ourselves as a "global Church." We have spent an inordinate amount of time and money trying to define ourselves in this image. The need for clear factual decision-making based on reality is critical. Until we admit there has been a spiritual revival going on around us while we have lost 30 percent of our membership, we will continue to make bad decisions.

We are not now nor have we ever been a global Church. Methodist globality is defined in the World Methodist Council. Outside the United States, there are only nine countries, all in Africa, with significant UM membership numbers. Of the 65 conferences outside the United States, only 11 qualify for more than the minimum of two delegates to General Conference, and approximately 25 have less than 5,000 members. In the remainder of the world outside southern Africa and the United States our total membership is around 250,000 in 39 conferences confined to parts of Europe and the Philippines. While serving as a District Governor of Rotary International, I learned what it is to be a global organization. Rotary has members in more than 200 countries. Rotary programs impact every (think 100 percent) country of the world. The parade of nations lasted for hours. That's global, and our Church doesn't even come close.

I believe a United States Central Conference (USCC) would result in irreversible division relatively quickly. Any group of Social Principles will be applicable nationally, not globally. To think otherwise is to denigrate the context of other nations. The idea that our Social Principles would be housed at the GC level over time may be one of those "things hoped for." There will be tremendous pressure to move responsibility for the Social Principles to the Central Conferences. This action would probably result in an undesirable change in the language relating to homosexuality, which would produce a justifiable separation as indicated in the text.

Further, the proposal provides for a new USCC College of Bishops as well as a new Committee on Episcopacy. Why these provisions if there is no plan to elect and assign episcopal leaders at the USCC? If we want membership to dramatically fall as it has in some jurisdictions, all we need do is follow a pattern of assigning episcopal leaders from declining jurisdictions to the stronger annual conferences.

Last fall, a Central Conference bishop stated to the Connectional Table that Central Conferences need to begin paying apportionments. Then he qualified it by saying it could not be much. The reality is that the United States provides 100 percent of the general Church funds. A USCC would cause this disparity to become even more controversial when voting on sharing funds.

Bishop Jones acknowledges that homogeneous ethnic churches are Christian in nature. So can denominational churches with homogeneous belief be Christian. I would submit that denominations with differing beliefs to the point of disharmony, mistrust, and constant bickering are by their very nature a discredit to Christianity. Pressure to keep these widely diverse denominations together must be questioned. If we are united, we do not need quick catch phrases and resolutions to know it. The desire in finding a solution is not to dominate but rather to stop the bleeding by eliminating the constant bickering over positions that are not going to change.

It's not the tolerance of different views that is at issue. It's our lack of mission! No group with significant differences in basic beliefs can ever reach its potential. Here, we are not talking about a disagreement over the wall color of the restrooms!

To partake of holy communion in a separated denomination will not change there being one loaf and one body sharing Christ. Most of us do not want separation, but our essential theological differences are not going away. The issue is not can we live with disunity, but how can we best live out our mission? Unity that is REAL is absolutely essential for any denomination to be successful in mission and ministry.

GERALD "JAY" WILLIAMS

Gift Receipt? Why Forced "Unity" in The United Methodist Church Must Be Rejected

Can the Church have a receipt with this gift of unity? It may want to exchange it for something better. The shirt does not fit. The sweater is itchy. Frankly, those shoes just are not the Church's type. "I appreciate the gift, please do not misunderstand me," she is saying, "but I would prefer something of my own choosing."

I agree with Bishop Jones, unity is a gift from God—one that we ought not be so arrogant to reject. Few would dispute that unity is part of the gospel mandate, and on a theological plane we affirm it. But the nature of unity in The United Methodist Church, as it has evolved over the past few quadrennia, has had little to do with this "means of grace." We have mistakenly spoken about spiritual unity without seriously considering the matters of power and justice that underlie our present (dis)unity. Rather, we speak of "unity" loosely as a code word masking our disagreement on homosexuality and biblical interpretation.

It is on this level of practice that I suggest unity ceases to be a gift from God and begins to be the product of broken people. And because the content and source of this "gift of unity" differ significantly from what Jones envisions as the balanced, extreme center stance of The United Methodist Church, I contend this unity is a gift not worth accepting in its current form. Let me be clear: The United Methodist Church does not experience the fullness of God's unity when it is bound together by a forced political unity.

Instead of trying to replace this gift, however, we must rather turn our attention to the Church's primary task of proclaiming and being good news in a world that needs the hope of Jesus Christ. As we interrogate our (dis)unity and remind ourselves of our brokenness, we might then embrace the foolishness of living in the gospel: God calls us even in our damaged form to be a gift to and a gift that transforms the world.

PRINCIPLE, PRACTICE, POWER, AND POLITICS

On the level of principle, Jones's argument and his analysis of unity, as laid out in Scripture and the apostolic tradition, is sound. The overarching Christian teachings on love, diversity, and inclusiveness disallow faithful disciples from concluding anything but God's desire for unity. Moreover, these teachings demand that Christians challenge hatred, uniformity, and exclusiveness in whatever forms and in whatever places they rear their ugly heads. This is what Jesus meant when he invited us to take up our crosses and follow him.

We need to remind ourselves that the "cross is something we can evade, but we nevertheless take it up willingly, even amid misgivings."[20] Most Christians agree that salvation and relationship to the Triune God is voluntary and not obligatory. Indeed Desmond Tutu is correct when he says, "God . . . has such a deep reverence for our freedom that [God] would much rather see us go freely to hell than compel us to go to heaven."[21] The cross, and thus our unity in the cross, is a choice and not a compulsion. Why then should our communal life in The United Methodist Church be any different?

Unfortunately though, on the level of practice, unity in The United Methodist Church, as expressed most recently in the 2000 and 2004 General Conferences, is maintained under the guise of political power and coercion and not in the spirit of choice and openness befitting of the gospel. As a member of the Faith and Order committee at the 2000 General Conference, I experienced firsthand how paralyzed our denomination has become by its legislative process. Though committee members shared honestly the ways Scripture, tradition, experience, and reason influenced their "position" on homosexuality, the culmination of our work was still a series of "up or down" votes on resolutions condoning or condemning homosexuality. Moreover, the sharing we experienced found no parallel in any of the deliberations in plenary sessions. By the end of those two weeks in Cleveland very little had changed. I am arguing that we needed—and still need—to be more open to hear the yearning of each other's hearts. I agree with Jones: "I welcome diverse opinions and conversation because I think the Church needs conversation."

Despite valiant attempts by the General Commission on Christian Unity and Interreligious Concerns to facilitate "Dialogues on Homosexuality," at a legislative level we fail to enter into serious conversation. When delegates left the 2004 General Conference without any substantial give-and-take, they had narrowed the Church's position by removing any linguistic ambiguity present in paragraph 304.3 and in the Social Principles of the 2000 *Book of Discipline*.[22]

General Conference voting trends on homosexuality illustrate the conservative/liberal sectarianism that divides the Church. Instead of becoming more open to dialogue around homosexuality or the role of Scripture, General Conference actions have done the opposite. The final issue of the *Daily Christian Advocate* of the 2004 General Conference reveals: "An attempt to add another sentence to the paragraph [161.G] recognizing that Christians disagree on the homosexuality issue was defeated . . . attempts to adjust language in paragraph 162.H, which deals with equal rights regardless of sexual orientation, were defeated by 2-1 margins."[23] Not only is one side "winning" the vote, but it is also prohibiting any official acknowledgment of theological positions alternative to that of the majority. In the absence of such recognition, our present denominational stance is not "balanced" as Jones suggests.

Although the 2004 General Conference also adopted the "unity resolution" as Jones highlights, I suggest the conference's stronger witness came through the above actions. Though we want to focus on the meaning of unity, secular media overwhelmingly reported about our infighting around sexuality. This is not an occasion where we can blame the media, however—we are entirely at fault. Instead of speaking about the gospel that liberates and heals, we spoke about our mess. The "unity resolution" was an afterthought once the denomination had already further concretized its prohibitive voice. Despite the positive symbolic sentimentality it gendered, the resolution was a palliative concession granted once

the political power of conservatives had been exercised. How do we genuinely talk about unity after the legislative decisions that reflect our disunity have been taken? Perhaps more important, how do we embrace
unity when we do not honestly discuss what divides us, or acknowledge
the minority report in our *Discipline?* Jones is correct, "The world needs a
united Church," but we offer division.

Few people genuinely desire Church schism as the "unity resolution"
affirmed. As Christians in the Wesleyan heritage we stay at the table.
With Jones, I maintain that the issue of homosexuality and others that
presently confront the Church, do not pass the tests that would necessi-
tate split. Every time our communions splinter, we betray the cross of
Christ and the Wesleyan movement that sought reform and revitaliza-
tion, not division.

Unity requires a coequality of parties. If we are to be a unified
Church, there must be an authentic willingness to live in community
with one another, not out of self-interest or even a mutual symbiosis,
but out of the *agape* love of Christ. Because most of us desire to stay at
the table under the will of Christ, when we deny genuine conversation—when we disallow ourselves from being "stretched" by what others propose—we coerce unity.

Hear me clearly: our present forced unity (i.e., disunity) is not simply
an indictment of the political power of conservatives. Stanley Hauerwas
states well, "Christian freedom lies in service, and Christian equality is
equality before God, and neither can be achieved through the coercive
efforts of liberal idealists who would transform the world into their
image."[24] To live in community requires both liberals and conservatives
to rely humbly on persuasion and not coercion to influence the Church's
voice.

The Church must never be a political confederation, guided by interest groups and sectarian agendas. Our unity should not flow from the fear
that schism would diminish our institutional size and stature, reducing
the power of our denomination, its episcopacy, general agencies, seminaries, and the like. Rather to embody Christian community is to be comfortable with the paradox of ambiguity; we realize that despite our

unworthiness God's grace calls us to reflect the unambiguous good news of God's love through Jesus Christ. In a word, Christian community is "dialectical"—characterized by a tensive yet holistic conversation. Despite the "unity resolution" we have to ask then: Why are we afraid to admit openly our lack of unanimity? It is only when we confess our dis-uniformity that we might live into our unity.

Our Methodist history ought to caution us. As a denomination we betrayed the gospel and Wesley's teaching before, regarding the issue of slavery. Though the 1784 Christmas Conference was decidedly antislavery, the 1836 General Conference took another stance. In Cincinnati the session "overwhelmingly adopted" resolutions that "first, the delegates 'disapprove in the most unqualified sense the conduct of two members of the General Conference, who are reported to have lectured in this city recently upon and in favour of modern abolitionism'; and second, that the delegates 'are decidedly opposed to modern abolitionism, and wholly disclaim any right, wish, or intention to interfere in the civil and political relation between master and slave as it exists in the slave-holding states of this union.'"[25] In hindsight we know that the General Conference action was unequivocally wrong in its censure and attempt to stymie debate on slavery and abolitionism. Might The United Methodist Church be committing again this folly of limiting truthful and justice-oriented discussion? We must wonder whether God's Word continues to be revealed in new ways each day and know that whenever we seek to close off dialogue, we may be blocking the good news.

SEEKING AND SPEAKING TRUTH

If nothing else, theological education has taught me that as Christians and as a Church we must not be too quick to "know" the will of God. Indeed the fullness of God's Word cannot be bound by our humanity. In this regard I hold Jones's statement that "The United Methodist General Conference discerns God's will" to be a bit presumptuous. Yes, as he continues, the General Conference establishes the denomination's discipline and doctrine, but I doubt that our committee meetings, parliamentary procedure, and plenary debates have anything to do with God's will for the Church.

United Methodist clergyman Christopher Morse's approach in *Not Every Spirit: A Dogmatics of Christian Disbelief* is helpful in our desire to be a faithful Church. Rooted in the admonition of 1 John 4:1 to "test the spirits," Morse challenges Christians to examine rigorously those things we claim to be true. He states, "If to believe in God is at the same time to disbelieve that which is not of God, every Christian confession of faith may be seen not only as affirming belief in God, but as entailing belief of what this faith in God refuses."[26] My faith in God rejects the powerful and coercive spirits—liberal or conservative—that seek to hinder conversation and monopolize the voice of "Christian teaching."

I am deeply indebted to Morse's framework as well as James Cone's prophetic voice, which reminds us that as "theologians of the church of Christ if we have difficulty telling the truth, then we ought to choose another profession. . . . We don't need people in the church who can't tell the truth."[27] Having tested the spirits, as Church leaders we must proclaim boldly the truth we find. It is not acceptable for us merely to recite what we have learned as children or received from other people. Instead we must seek and know the truth for ourselves.

It seems to me that the "extreme center" that Jones suggests is possible, but only when in seeking and speaking these truths we realize with humility that we cannot have all the answers. In fact, the more we seek to know about God, the less we know. This is part of the mystery, which is the foolishness of the gospel (1 Corinthians 1–3). We are never coerced by the gospel, only persuaded. But in order to be transformed, as Christians we must first be willing. As a Church we cannot force unity—we can only invite it through open dialogue and Christian communion. Yes, unity is a gift from God. But the compulsory "unity" we presently experience in The United Methodist Church, characterized by political maneuvering and deadened dialogue, is not of God—it is of our own making. And as such, it is not a gift worth keeping. Next time, the Church might be better served with a gift card.

WILLIAM H. WILLIMON

Unity in Christ

A major historic ministry of bishops is to be a sign of the unity of the body of Christ at the Lord's Table. In appealing for unity, Scott Jones is fulfilling the historic function of the bishop. Scott goes about his call for unity in the right way—with wonderfully Wesleyan theological authorization. The only good reasons for staying unified as a Church are christological. The only means of being unified are christological. The organizational unity of the Church rests upon a theological claim of who Jesus is and what Jesus does. As Bishop Jones has said, unity is a gift that the risen Christ gives to the Church.

True, like the resurrection itself, our unity is both a present reality and future expectation. We are not fully unified yet. (I figure about a third of Paul's letters, and maybe as much of the Gospels, minister to the Church's disunity.) When Jesus was raised from the dead, he began bringing an odd assortment of people together. First, Jew and Jew (Acts 2), then Jew and Gentile (Acts 10:45), and then every nation upon the earth (Matthew 28). So those who first testified gave witness not only to their belief that crucified Jesus was raised from the dead but also to their experience that the risen Christ got people in sync. This is miraculous work, something that only a unified, unifying Trinitarian God could pull off. With so many divisions, the unity that Christ gives is yet another sign of Christ's victory. In a world at war, where divisions predominate, if anyone is able to look at any church, anywhere that truly demonstrates unity, this is visible testimony of the miracle of the resurrection.

In this theological claim is also an organizational warning. Woe unto the church that attempts to make unity the result of savvy organization or earnest human striving. The unity of the Church is a theological rather than a sociological phenomenon. As Scott puts it, this is to be "received rather than achieved." The world's primary means of achieving unity is through coercion—social, military, or legislative coercion. (We're going to make a united Iraq if we have to devastate the whole desert to deliver it.)

One of the challenges of the unity that Christ brings is that it is often a unity that is unrecognizable to the world. Scott suggests this in stating that "God does not intend uniformity." In the world, unity is synonymous with uniformity. The conventional modern means of achieving uniformity is through bureaucracy. Bureaucracy is authoritarianism that hides its coercion behind impersonally administered rules and regulations—a nameless, faceless, boringly gray mass of uniformity. The world touts "diversity," which becomes another form of loneliness—you stay out of my life and I promise to stay out of yours and we'll call that "justice." I have my peculiarities and you have yours, which is beautiful as long as you remain detached and distant from me in exchange for my staying a stranger to you.

Christians are not called to practice diversity or pluralism or inclusivism or tolerance (the world's pitiful, groping attempts to deal with the reality of difference). Christians are called by Christ *to love*. Jesus never asked us to be sensitive to the stranger. We are to receive the stranger, to love the stranger as Christ loves, to discipline ourselves to call the stranger "brother," "sister," even commanded to love our enemies. Thus the Church has a more complicated notion of unity than that which passes for unity in the Republican Party.

Unity in Christ is unity that is congruent with a God who is triune. It is of the nature of the trinitarian God to be a complex, real unity that is formed of real diversity. Father, Son, and Holy Spirit are truly one and are yet truly distinctive as three ways of being the same God. In the world, unity means forced uniformity, diversity means tolerated difference, and most live in unbridgeable separation because the world does not yet know a God who is Father, Son, and Holy Spirit. As Charles Wesley put it in a hymn, "These Three Are One."

I am troubled that in the last couple of decades our Church has tried to have unity the world's way, rather than God's way, to achieve through legislative coercion that which the gospel did not deliver. Why is it a threat to my church in Alabama if United Methodists in California organize themselves differently from my annual conference? God gives special missions to each of us; why can't we vibrantly and distinctively respond to the mission God gives? A succession of recent General Conferences rendered us into a brittle, unresponsive, overly structured organization. We have thus aggravated the problem of disunity.

For instance, as chair of the General Conference Commission on Ministry, I worry that we are increasingly taking away the responsibility for the training, examination, and ordaining of persons to the United Methodist ministry from the annual conference and giving it to the General Conference. Clergy sexuality issues have taken too large a place, and clergy productivity and effectiveness issues have taken too small a place in our conversation. Given a culture in which sexuality has become the supreme defining characteristic of human beings, the way the world tries to organize itself (the "Gay Community," the "Hispanic Community"), should we give the world's way of organizing human beings, so much weight in Christ's church?

I have envied those churches that enjoy a more easily defined, coherent, and concise theology and practice of ordained ministry. Ask an Anglican what her church believes about the ordering of ministry, and you will probably get an orderly reply. Our sometimes competing, diverse practices of ministry seem to arise out of competing ecclesiologies and move in different directions at once.

And yet I have learned to see some of this apparent messiness as an aspect of our Wesleyan determination to reach out to the world in the name of Christ and to be half as expansive as Christ in convening a church in his name.

Special interest groups—whether they are the Institute on Religion and Democracy or Affirmation—love their one issue (usually homosexuality) more than they love the unity of the Church. Shouting slogans past one another, they fail to engage in Wesleyan "Christian conferencing," because real conversation requires a willingness to encounter the other as another and to the possibility of being changed by the other in the conversation. One of the ways that Jesus Christ is Lord is by making enemies into friends. Thus for one Christian to say to another, "that you and I disagree on this issue necessitates separation" is to raise troubling christo-logical questions. Can Jesus give what he promises?

Woe unto the church that attempts to coerce unity, hoping to achieve with the law what only gospel can do. I pray that one day General Conference might refrain from all legislation—not offer or pass a single resolution, law, rule, or mandate. Just gather, sing, pray, report on what good we've done and left undone, and see if the Holy Spirit might descend upon us and shake us up. That would be "Christian conferenc-ing" worthy of the name.

Christology accounts for my only reservation about Scott's most salubri-ous teaching on unity. Critics said many things about Jesus, but no one ever accused him of being in the middle of anything, except controversy. Jesus and centrist just don't seem to go together. Scott says he doesn't mean a "dead center." While I see the need of calling the Christian center the "extreme" center, it's still the center, implying that somewhere within the Christian faith there is that form of orthodoxy that is somehow closer to the real truth of things, at the center of things. The "extreme center" also implies that our trouble with disunity would be solved if we could somehow silence or neutralize all those fanatics who shout from the margins and the edges at those of us who have at last discovered the true center.

Jesus was eccentric in welcoming to himself those whom the world had pushed to the margins. In fact, the way I read the Gospels, it was often those wild, outspoken ones on the margins who first recognized Jesus as the Christ. This implies that we ought to be suspicious of those agreeable moderates who think they are at the center and to try to listen to those fanatics on the edge. Unity in Christ is more than simply finding some safe, tranquil middle ground on which to stand with as many people as possible. Rather, Christian unity means learning to love and to make Eucharist with those whom Christ has called to himself. As a follower of Jesus, I don't have to like them, approve of them, or agree with them. I just have to love them as Christ has loved me. This is what makes being with Christ, at the center, so extremely challenging and also extremely gratifying—loving those whom Christ has extremely loved. "You did not choose me but I chose you" (John 15:16).

I don't believe that we need to uncover and to agree on some center of essential doctrines and assertions. We need to keep Christ as the center, to keep trying to love him as he has loved us, to keep close to his way with the world, treating our enemies and those who are strangers to us as he treated them and treats us.

Scott notes that congregations must reach out across cultural divides and reach people for Christ. Good. But we are inviting people, in Christ's name, to join his rag-tag assortment of disciples, the called out, The United Methodist Church, for whom he is the center. And the historical Jesus was noted, and frequently criticized, perhaps even crucified, because of his propensity to leave the official center and reach out to the margins to form a new family constituted by those who were often excluded by those at the center.

Scott's stress on Methodism as missional and unity for the sake of and as the fruit of mission seems just right. If we would worry more about mission, if we would confess the ways in which our internal disputes and factionalism sap the energies from our Christ mandated mission, we would be more faithful.

Keeping clear about our mission, I believe that we would be more unified in Christ. I have congregations in my conference that have so little to do (other than to look after their internal needs) that they have enough time to split up into factions and fight it out among themselves. Fortunately, I also have congregations who have recovered the adventure of being the body of Christ in motion, and have had their internal problems put in proper perspective, by engaging in costly, risky, life-giving mission with Christ. I know once sick, self-centered, peevish, declining congregations that were born again by simply evangelizing enough new people whose presence among them made their past differences among themselves look petty and trivial.

Scott's stress on the mission of Christ is the way forward.

DAVID K. YEMBA

I am glad to have this opportunity offered graciously by Bishop Scott J. Jones to respond to his essay timely titled "God's Gift of Unity for United Methodism." In fact the book is a call to all United Methodists: clergy and laity, men and women, older and younger, conservative and liberal to begin a serious conversation within the denomination on the precious gift of God's unity. The author states the main purpose of the book in these terms:

> While most of my views are applicable to Christians generally, I wish to speak specifically to my own Church with reference to our own issues. In preparation for the General Conference in 2008, but also in preparation for the entire future of the Church, I hope to suggest wherein our unity lies and some ideas of how we might live more fully into God's gift of unity.

> But I seek not only to talk about unity but also to model it.

Therefore it is in response to this immediate invitation of Bishop Jones, but also the desire to engage in this important conversation that I have accepted to put together some thoughts from an African context. My response will reflect the experience of my involvement in the ecumenical movement at a multilateral dialogue level, but also the experience from my own episcopal area in the Congo.

The first merit of this book is the simplicity of the language that the author has used. The text does not target a group or category of people within United Methodism. Rather, it introduces the issue of unity and at the same time the passion of the author for unity. It seeks ways of defining and modeling this unity in bringing together views to discuss them in the light of biblical witness and Wesleyan tradition. As an introduction to the specific issue of unity in United Methodism, the text is relatively short and on the target. Many United Methodists will find "God's Gift of Unity for United Methodism" informative and to some extent will get sufficiently introduced to issues that threaten the unity of the denomination at this beginning of the twenty-first century.

The second merit of this book is the priority Bishop Jones has given to the mission of the Church in the search of Christian unity. The approach sounds both biblical and Wesleyan. As stated in the text, the Church does not exist for its own sake:

> United Methodism lives by its mission. We were not founded in doctrinal dispute. . . . When we are clear about our mission, we thrive. When we are confused about our mission or when we adopt a partial mission in place of the whole gospel, we die.

The Church exists as an instrument of God's mercy to humanity on one hand and as an instrument to bring this humanity and the whole creation into communion with God on the other hand. Therefore, the mission of the Church as the body of Christ consists of the continuation of the mission of Jesus Christ in the world. This is clear from the beginning of Jesus' ministry:

> "The Spirit of the Lord is upon me,
>   because he has anointed me
>   to bring good news to the poor.
> He has sent me to proclaim release to the captives
>   and recovery of sight to the blind,
>   to let the oppressed go free,
> to proclaim the year of the Lord's favor." (Luke 4:18-19)

However, the mission of the Church is discussed here in the context of the three "necessary elements of unity" in the book, together with discipline and doctrine. One would expect to get some clarification whether the three essential elements—mission, discipline, and doctrine—are discussed in the order of priority. In the quotation of *The Works of John Wesley* (Jackson Edition 13:258), John Wesley said the following about Methodists:

> unless they hold fast both the doctrine, spirit and discipline with which they first set out.

In this quotation, the doctrine comes before the discipline. As to the content of the mission of the Church, the doctrine or the teaching of the faith of the Church comes before the organization. The connectional system of our Church and the place conference occupies in our polity are no doubt some of the essential ingredients for Christian Unity. However, because of its close relations with the faith of the Church through the ages, the doctrine would mean more to unity than discipline. In fact this is well reflected in the text, especially when unity is discussed from a single Christian Church perspective:

> But there is also the matter of unity within a single Christian Church. There, we must have agreement in essential doctrine, a common mission and a common discipline.

But the priority of the doctrine over the discipline leads to a deeper consideration. While I totally agree with Bishop Jones in his analysis of the Catholic Spirit according to John Wesley, the title of this section may be misleading: "Diversity in Unity: Catholic Spirit." The unity is a gift of God to the Church. It is this gift that throws light on diversity within the life of our Church. The recent ecumenical studies have shown that the unity we seek is both a gift and calling (see particularly John 17:21-23). The oneness of the Church is the gift of the triune God which has to be put in action in the diversity of gifts the Holy Spirit bestows in the body of Christ, in the diversity of Church members in their geographical and cultural settings. The catholic spirit would therefore be the result of the spirit of unity in diversity. In any case, this could just be a matter of methodology.

In the same section, the Church is considered, as a means of grace, a sacrament. It is important to point out at this stage of internal conversation on the gift of unity for United Methodists, that the issue of Church as a "Sacrament" is still a divisive issue in the ecumenical circles. If our Church moves to the position of taking the church as sacrament, then we will need to clarify the relation between this sacrament and the sacraments of baptism and the Lord's Supper/holy communion. The churches who do not take the Church as a sacrament consider the sacraments as: "the means of salvation, through which Christ sustains the church, and not actions by which the church realizes or actualizes itself."[28]

Areas of diversity and limits of diversity are clearly balanced in the text. This will certainly help our congregations and annual conferences foster the sentiment of seeking unity in our cultural diversities. It should be noted that in African languages, for instance, there is no distinctions between pronouns "he" and "she." The same word is also used for "him" and "her." The use of the same word to call men and women should at least in an African context help reflect more deeply on relationship between men and women in the Church as well as in the society.

The Church's teaching on the issue of homosexuality is a hot potato in Western culture today. It has some impact on other cultures too. The issue has political, legal, and religious implications. At this stage of discussion on this burning issue, it is important to judge every position in the light of God's love, avoiding extreme positions. The Church's radical position must be to love our brother and sister as ourselves. Bishop Jones is right to say that he does "not regard our teaching on homosexuality as an essential doctrine." In saying so, he neither closes the door for conversation nor gives an added value to this issue.

It is my hope that this essay will meet the expectations of those United Methodists who are eager to seek unity of the Church of God locally, regionally, and globally.

Unity is essential not only for the mission or the apostolicity of the Church but also for the Christian understanding of the glory of God. The Church is not only one, it is also holy. When Jesus prayed for the oneness of his disciples so that the world may believe in him, he also related the unity to the glory of God in his prayer:

> The glory that you have given me I have given them, so that they may be one as we are one. I in them and you in me, that they may become completely one, so that the world may know that you have sent me and have loved them even as you have loved me. (John 17:22-23)

The Church has received the glory of God by Jesus Christ, the Son of God, and therefore it is, by the power of the Holy Spirit, the body of Christ (Ephesians 1:23; 2:16), the people of God (1 Peter 2:9-10) and the temple of the Holy Spirit (1 Peter 2:5; Ephesians 2: 21-22). Thus the people so defined and identified are continually called:

to lead a life worthy of the calling to which you have been called, with all humility and gentleness, with patience, bearing with one another in love, making every effort to maintain the unity of the Spirit in the bond of peace. (Ephesians 4:1b-3)

It is a privilege for us people called United Methodists, like all other Christians, to become participants in building the unity of the Christian church. For that reason, let us always, even in tensions, remember that we are the people called to give glory to the Holy One in our efforts toward Christian unity and the holiness of Christian life.

To him be glory in the church and in Christ Jesus to all generations, forever and ever. Amen. (Ephesians 3:21)

CHAPTER THREE

SCOTT JONES'S RESPONSE TO THE CONVERSATION

I n many places I have led audiences in repeating an important phrase: "the main thing is to keep the main thing the main thing." Doing so leads people to ask "What is the main thing?" and then to focus their time, talents, and money on the purpose for which the Church exists. I believe unity is an important part of the "main thing." Living into the gift of unity requires focus on our deepest purpose and what God is doing in our midst.

I offer three observations after reading all of the responses. First, I believe that many of the tensions present in our Church today receive clear presentation in this conversation. Some believe that unity is valuable, but justice (their version of it) is more important. Some believe that unity is valuable, but doubt that unity can be achieved with such wide diversity of practice. Others prefer to live with hope that Christ's body is big enough to include a wide variety of persons who can be united around a common doctrine, mission, and discipline. While I belong to this middle group, such a position demands clarity with regard to both the goal and the means to attain it. This conversation has added to my awareness of the difficulties of my own position.

Second, conversations like this one can help by naming the issues involved. Sometimes they show ways to resolve the tensions or to move forward while living with them. Whether this book does so will be made clear in those places where it fosters helpful conversations within The United Methodist Church.

Third, I still believe that God and the world need a united United Methodist Church and that my basic approach holds the best promise for that. I might summarize this approach as placing a high value on unity for biblical, theological, and missional reasons, and defining unity in doctrinal, spiritual, and missional terms. This does not mean uniformity, and the variety of voices represented in this book show how much we all need one another to discern God's will for our Church.

I believe this volume shows the advantages of diversity. Those who disagreed with me pointed up deficiencies in my position. Those who agreed with me often added new insights or better ways of communicating the points I was trying to express. The value of our diversity is evident herein.

However, the question that is not adequately addressed in this volume is what are the legitimate boundaries of that diversity? At what point should people be invited to come closer to the center of the Church lest they fall off the edge?

I believe the concluding question of my essay, "How do we live more fully into this gift of unity?" is not susceptible of an easily formulated, once-for-all answer. Rather, it is a guiding question worth asking, answering, and then asking again. God is calling us to unity, mission, and embodying "the faith that was once for all entrusted to the saints" (Jude 3). May God continue to guide the people of The United Methodist Church.

NOTES

Preface

1. William Butler Yeats, "The Second Coming," used by permission of AP Watt Ltd on behalf of Gráinne Yeats. Reprinted with the permission of Scribner, an imprint of Simon & Schuster Adult Publishing Group, from THE COLLECTED WORKS OF W.B. YEATS, VOLUME I: THE POEMS, Revised, edited by Richard J. Finneran. Copyright © 1924 by The Macmillan Company; copyright renewed © 1952 by Bertha Georgie Yeats. All rights reserved.

1. God's Gift of Unity for United Methodism

1. *Daily Christian Advocate*, vol. 4, number 11, published May 8, 2004, page 2250. The five delegates jointly making the motion were Kristina J. Gonzalez, Jon R. Gray, Mary Alice Massey, Beatrice Fofonah, Luis F. Reyes, and John Schol.

2. "In Search of Unity" (New York: General Commission on Christian Unity and Interreligious Concerns, 1998).

3. "In Search of Unity," p. 3.

4. The Nicene Creed, *The United Methodist Hymnal* (Nashville: The United Methodist Publishing House, 1989), 880.

5. Stephen Rhodes has helped me understand this text in juxtaposition with the Tower of Babel Story in Genesis 9. He argues that diversity is God's plan and that this theme runs through the entire Scripture. See his *Where the Nations Meet: The Church in a Multicultural World* (Downers Grove, Ill.: Intervarsity Press, 1998).

6. David Bosch, *Transforming Mission: Paradigm Shifts in Theology of Mission*, American Society of Missiology Series, No. 16 (Maryknoll, N.Y.: Orbis Books, 1991), 30.

7. "Upon our Lord's Sermon on the Mount, V," *The Works of John Wesley*, vol. 1, *Sermons* I: 1–33, ed. Albert C. Outler (Nashville: Abingdon Press, 1989), §II.2-3, 554-55.

8. The Nicene Creed.

9. For examples, see David Bosch, *Transforming Mission*; Darrell Guder et al., *Missional Church: A Vision for the Sending of the Church in North America* (Grand Rapids, Mich. and Cambridge, U.K.: Eerdmans, 1998); and William J. Abraham, *The Logic of Evangelism* (Grand Rapids, Mich.: Eerdmans, 1989).

10. Carlos Cardoza-Orlandi, *Mission: An Essential Guide* (Nashville: Abingdon Press, 2002), 42.

11. See my *Evangelistic Love of God and Neighbor* (Nashville: Abingdon Press, 2003) for a discussion of seven aspects of discipleship and why belonging and actively participating in the life of a congregation are essential to Christian discipleship.

12. *Grace Given to You in Christ: Catholics and Methodists Reflect Further on the Church*, Report of the Joint International Commission for Dialogue between the World Methodist Council and the Roman Catholic Church (Seoul, 2006). The citation is from the Commission's *Speaking the Truth in Love* (Brighton, 2001), §28.

13. Jim Collins, *Good to Great: Why Some Companies Make the Leap . . . And Others Don't* (New York: HarperBusiness, 2001), 86.

14. "Thoughts upon Methodism," *The Works of John Wesley*, vol. 13, ed. Thomas Jackson (London: Wesleyan Conference Office, 1872; repr., Grand Rapids, Mich.: Zondervan, 1958–1959), 258.

15. These are real congregations. One of them has changed its sense of mission and started growing.

16. "Causes of the Inefficacy of Christianity," *Works*, vol. 4, *Sermons IV*: 115–151, ed. Outler, §7, 90.

17. *The United Methodist Hymnal* (Nashville: The United Methodist Publishing House, 1989), 38.

18. John Wesley, *Explanatory Notes upon the New Testament* (London: William Bowyer, 1755; repr. London: Wesleyan-Methodist Book Room, n.d.), Romans 12:6.

19. "Little Gidding" in FOUR QUARTERS, copyright 1942 by T.S. Eliot and renewed 1970 by Esme Valerie Eliot, reprinted with the permission of Harcourt, Inc.

20. "The Way to the Kingdom," *Works*, vol. 10, ed. Jackson, 72.22. Brian McLaren, *A Generous Orthodoxy* (Grand Rapids, Mich.: Zondervan, 2004), 14.

21. McLaren, *Generous Orthodoxy*, 14.

22. "The Way to the Kingdom," *Works*, vol. 1, *Sermons I*: 1–33, ed. Outler, §I.6, 220-21.

23. My list of "Ten Things Every Christian Ought to Know (from a United Methodist Point of View)" with a brief explanation and relevant hymns is at www.extremecenter.org. A longer explanation and detailed discussion of United Methodist doctrine is in my *United Methodist Doctrine: The Extreme Center*.

24. "Catholic Spirit," *Works*, vol. 2, *Sermons II*: 34–70, ed. Outler, §1, 3–4, 81-82.

25. Ibid., §III.4, 94.

26. See Stephen Rhodes, *Where the Nations Meet*, for a stronger argument about how multicultural congregations exemplify God's plan for the church.

27. *Grace Given to You in Christ: Catholics and Methodists Reflect Further on the Church*, Report of the Joint International Commission for Dialogue between the World Methodist Council and the Roman Catholic Church (Seoul, 2006). The quotation is from Archbishop Rowan Williams, Address at the Signing of an Anglican-Methodist Covenant, Westminster, England, 1 November, 2003.

28. "On Schism," *Works*, vol. 3, *Sermons III*: 71–114, ed. Outler, §II.10, 64.

29. Ibid.

30. Ibid., 67.

31. Ibid.

32. "In Search of Unity," 3.

33. "In Search of Unity," 5-11.

34. See *Explanatory Notes Upon the New Testament*, Revelation 17:10, and my comments on this passage in *United Methodist Doctrine: The Extreme Center*, 62.

35. For helpful background see Ted Campbell, "The 'Wesleyan Quadrilateral': The Story of a Modern Methodist Myth" in Thomas A. Langford, ed., *Doctrine and Theology in the United Methodist Church* (Nashville: Abingdon Press, 1991), 154-61.

36. Stephen Gunter et al., *Wesley and the Quadrilateral*, 42.

37. *Explanatory Notes Upon the New Testament*, Romans 12:6.

38. *The United Methodist Hymnal*, 9-10.

39. Ibid., 88.

40. "In Search of Unity," 7.

41. *The United Methodist Hymnal*, 11.

2. Responses to "God's Gift of Unity"

1. Rabbinical Assembly website, Press release, December 6, 2006, www.rabbin icalassembly.org/press/docs/CJLS

2. Rabbinical Assembly website, www.rabbinicalassembly.org/law/contemporary_halakhah.html

3. Preached at Claremont United Methodist Church on the occasion of their tenth anniversary of becoming a Reconciling Congregation, May 18, 2003.

4. Melanie Morrison, *The Grace of Coming Home: Spirituality, Sexuality, and the Struggle for Justice* (Cleveland: Pilgrim Press, 1995), 25.

5. Lyle Schaller, *The Ice Cube Is Melting* (Nashville: Abingdon Press, 2004).

6. James A. Harnish, *You Only Have to Die* (Nashville: Abingdon Press, 2004).

7. S. L. Gaertner and J. F. Dovidio, "The Aversive Form of Racism" in: J. F. Dovidio and S. L. Gaertner, eds., *Prejudice, Discrimination and Racism: Theory and Research* (Orlando, Fla.: Academic Press, 1986), 61-89.

8. The General Conference of the UMC: *Daily Christian Advocate*: Daily Report, vol. 4, no. 11 Saturday, May 8, 2004, pages 2149ff., also The Round-Up Edition, May 8, 2004, pages 2337f.; *New York Times*, Friday, May 7, 2007.

9. Reported in the *Pittsburgh Press*, June 15, 1991.

10. Jones, 61.

11. See more of my story in *Loyal Opposition*, editors Tex Sample and Amy DeLong, (Nashville: Abingdon Press, 2000) or *Voices from the Kingdom*, Beverly Cole (Salina, Kans.: Kimimi Publications, 2007).

12. "The Character of a Methodist," *The Works of John Wesley*, vol. 9, *The Methodist Societies: History, Nature, and Design*, ed. Rupert E. Davies (Nashville: Abingdon Press, 1989), §1, 33.

13. Ibid., §1, 33-34.

14. Ibid., §16, 41.

15. Ibid., §17, 41.

16. The Confessing Movement within The United Methodist Church, "What Is The Confessing Movement within The United Methodist Church" (Indianapolis: Confessing Movement, 1995).

17. "The Confessing Statement: We Confess Jesus Christ: The Son, The Savior, The Lord," The Confessing Movement within The United Methodist Church,

http://confessingumc.org/v2/resources/confession.htm, dated April 29, 1995 (accessed June 13, 2007).

18. "Unity in Christ, That the World May Believe," The Confessing Movement Conference, http://confessingumc.org/v2/2005Unity Statement.htm (accessed June 13, 2007).

19. George Thomas Kurian, David B. Barrett, and Todd M. Johnson, *World Christian Encyclopedia: A Comparative Survey of Churches and Religions in the Modern World* (Oxford: Oxford University Press, 2001).

20. Laurence Hull Stookey, *This Day: A Wesleyan Way of Prayer* (Nashville: Abingdon Press, 2004), 27.

21. Peter Storey, *Listening at Golgotha* (Nashville: Upper Room Books, 2004), 33.

22. In several arenas the denomination's position on homosexuality was challenged on the basis of disciplinary word choice. Most notably in the clergy trial of Reverend Karen Dammann the statement "Since the practice of homosexuality is incompatible with Christian teaching, self-avowed practicing homosexuals are not to be accepted as candidates, ordained as ministers, or appointed to serve in The United Methodist Church" (*2000 Book of Discipline* ¶304.3) was deemed not to be enforceable because it was based on the Social Principles, which is a teaching document and not church law (see its preamble). The 2004 General Conference responded by not only editing the Social Principles but also rephrasing the church's stance to be a stand-alone statement of church law to say: "The practice of homosexuality is incompatible with Christian teaching. Therefore, self-avowed practicing homosexuals are not to be certified as candidates, ordained as ministers, or appointed to serve in The United Methodist Church" (*2004 Book of Discipline* ¶304.3). In no uncertain terms, the legislative body made clear that its prohibitive sentiments on homosexuality and ordination of gays and lesbians would not be dismissed because of technicalities in wording.

23. 2004 General Conference *Daily Christian Advocate* (Volume 5, May 8, 2004): 2338-39.

24. Stanley Hauerwas, "The Servant Community: Christian Social Ethics" in *The Hauerwas Reader*, John Berkman and Michael Cartwright, eds. (Durham: Duke University Press, 2001), 389.

25. H. Shelton Smith, *In His Image, But . . . : Racism in Southern Religion, 1780–1910* (Durham: Duke University Press, 1972), 101.

26. Christopher Morse, *Not Every Spirit: A Dogmatics of Christian Disbelief* (Harrisburg: Trinity Press International, 1994), 13.

27. James Cone, "The Vocation of a Theologian," *Union News* (Winter 1991): 4.

28. *The Nature and Mission of the Church. A Stage on the Way to a Common Statement*, Faith and Order, Paper no. 198, WCC, 2005, 29.

CONTRIBUTORS

William J. Abraham, Albert Cook Outler Professor of Wesley Studies and Altshuler Distinguished Teaching Professor, Perkins School of Theology, Southern Methodist University, Dallas, Texas; and clergy member of the Southwest Texas Annual Conference.

Lonnie D. Brooks, retired oil exploration geophysicist, member of East Anchorage United Methodist Church, Anchorage, Alaska, Adult Sunday School Teacher.

Mary Brooke Casad, Director of Connectional Ministries, North Texas Conference, member of Christ United Methodist Church, Farmers Branch, Texas.

Amy DeLong, Executive Director of Kairos CoMotion, member of Wisconsin Annual Conference serving in Extension Ministry.

Sudarshana Devadhar, Resident Bishop New Jersey Area, The United Methodist Church.

Sally Dyck, Resident Bishop Minnesota Area, The United Methodist Church.

James A. Harnish, Senior Pastor Hyde Park United Methodist Church, Tampa, Florida, Florida Annual Conference.

Carolyn E. Johnson, Director of Diversity, Purdue University, a member of the Imagine Indiana Core Group and a member of St. Andrew United Methodist Church, West Lafayette, Indiana.

Scott J. Jones, Resident Bishop Kansas Area, The United Methodist Church.

Susan J. Laurie, Outreach Coordinator for Reconciling Ministries Network (RMN) and member of United Church of Rogers Park (UMC), Chicago, Illinois.

Bill McAlilly, Seashore District Superintendent, Mississippi Conference, The United Methodist Church.

Patricia L. Miller, Indiana State Senator and Executive Director of The Confessing Movement within The United Methodist Church, and member of Old Bethel United Methodist Church, Indianapolis, Indiana.

John R. Schol, Resident Bishop Washington, D.C. Area, The United Methodist Church.

Joe M. Whittemore, member of Hartwell First United Methodist Church in the North Georgia Annual Conference and Connectional Table of The United Methodist Church.

Gerald "Jay" Williams, member of Metropolitan United Methodist Church, Affiliate Member of Metropolitan Community United Methodist Church.

William H. Willimon, Resident Bishop Birmingham Area, The United Methodist Church.

David K. Yemba, Resident Bishop Central Congo Central Conference, The United Methodist Church.